The Tommy Keene
Handbook

The Tommy Keene Handbook

✦

A Comprehensive Guide to the Music of Tommy Keene

Geoff Cabin

iUniverse, Inc.
New York Lincoln Shanghai

The Tommy Keene Handbook
A Comprehensive Guide to the Music of Tommy Keene

iUniverse books may be ordered through booksellers or by contacting:

iUniverse
2021 Pine Lake Road, Suite 100
Lincoln, NE 68512
www.iuniverse.com
1-800-Authors (1-800-288-4677)

ISBN: 978-0-595-44770-1 (pbk)
ISBN: 978-0-595-89089-7 (ebk)

Printed in the United States of America

Contents

I. Musical History

Introduction

For more than 20 years, Tommy Keene has been one of the leading creative forces in pop and rock music. Starting with the release of his first album in 1982, Keene has released a series of albums and EPs that contain some of the best pop and rock music ever produced, featuring songs with introspective and reflective lyrics and buoyant pop melodies, backed by hard-rocking rhythms and Keene's electrifying guitar playing. Keene also has toured extensively and proven himself to be a dynamic and energetic performer. While Keene has never achieved great commercial success or widespread recognition, he has produced a body of work that places him squarely in the ranks of the greatest pop and rock artists.

Early Days: The Rage, Razz, and the Pieces

Tommy Keene was born on June 30, 1958 in the Chicago, Illinois area, and grew up in Bethesda, Maryland, a suburb of Washington, D.C.[1] Keene became involved in music at an early age. One of his earliest memories is seeing the Beatles on *The Ed Sullivan Show* when he was four and a half years old.[2] Around the same time, Keene began playing the piano.[3] "I started off playing the piano," he recalled. "I was, I guess, about four. And I was playing classical piano until about age eight. My teacher stopped giving lessons for health reasons. And then I took up the drums and guitar."[4] Keene also started attending concerts while still a pre-teen. "… I saw a lot of shows at a very young age," he remembered. "My dad took my brother and me to my first concert when I was eight, the Dave Clark Five in 1967, and the opening act was Neil Diamond. Then we saw the Buffalo Springfield and the Beach Boys. I saw the Who in 1968, with the Troggs opening … Soon as my older brother got his license, we were off and running, driving to New York and Philadelphia to see everybody."[5]

While attending junior high school, Keene joined his first real band, Blue Steel.[6] Initially the band was a four-piece that consisted of Keene on drums, Victor Coelho on guitar, Mike Lofgren on guitar, and John Stasio on bass.[7] The band changed to a three-piece with the departure of Mike Lofgren and John Stasio and the addition of Vince Corvelli on bass.[8] The group did covers of songs by Alice Cooper, Deep Purple, Rory Gallagher, and the Who, among others.[9] "We got into the English glam thing totally, did lots of Mott the Hoople," Keene stated.[10]

While in high school, Keene made the transition to lead guitarist as part of a group called Only After Dark.[11] "That was some friends of my older brother, who he was going to University of Maryland with," Keene explained. "They were from Hagerstown, and we used to play a bunch of, I guess, clubs or teen clubs in Hagerstown … I sort of learned the ropes on guitar in that group … It was a cover band. We were doing Lou Reed and Mott the Hoople and David Bowie and Bruce Springsteen. Stuff like that, stuff that was popular that we liked at the time."[12]

After graduating from high school, Keene attended the University of Maryland at College Park. In the fall of his sophomore year in 1977, he met Richard X. Heyman and they formed a group called the Rage.[13] Heyman is a native of New Jersey who had played in a group called the Doughboys before moving to Maryland.[14] In the Rage, Heyman sang lead and played rhythm guitar while Keene played lead guitar.[15] The group also included Ricky Street on bass and Jim Dougherty on drums.[16]

Heyman was already an accomplished songwriter, and the Rage performed his songs as well as covers of sixties-era songs.[17] The group played in a pop-rock style that drew heavily on the sounds of the British Invasion of the mid-sixties. "We had this whole *schtick* down with our Beatle-y outfits," Keene related. "We were different. Nobody in D.C. was doing that, although in L.A., the Pop, 20/20, and the Knack were happening simultaneously."[18]

Although the Rage was primarily a vehicle for Heyman's songs, Keene also began to write songs around this time. "I'd just started to write songs," Keene recalled. "In fact my big song in the Rage was 'Love Is Love' and I think I had one other song, I can't even remember the name of it … But that ['Love Is Love'] was sort of the first song that I had written that I thought was kind of decent."[19]

The Rage often opened shows at the Varsity Grill Back Room for D.C.'s top rock band at the time—Razz.[20] By 1977, Razz already had a long history behind it. The band had originally formed in 1970, had undergone numerous personnel changes, and had broken up and reformed a couple of times.[21] (For a comprehensive history of Razz, see *Capitol Rock* by Mark Opsasnick [www.capitol-rock.com].)

After a hiatus during 1976, Razz regrouped in early 1977 with a lineup that consisted of Michael Reidy on vocals, Abaad Behram on guitar, Bill Craig on guitar, Ted Niceley on bass, and Doug Tull on drums.[22] At this time the band began to concentrate on original material, written by Reidy and Behram.[22] Razz started gigging again the the spring of 1977, and during the following year they established themselves as a major draw at clubs in the Washington, D.C. area, made out-of-town forays to play places such as Baltimore and New York, and began receiving favorable press from publications such as *The Unicorn Times* and *The Washington Post*.[24] In February 1978, Razz further established their reputation as a leading local band with the release of their first single, "C. Redux" b/w "Seventies Anomie" on the local O'Rourke label.[25]

In May 1978, Abaad Behram quit Razz.[26] (Behram joined the power pop band Artful Dodger, and subsequently formed his own group, Johnny Bombay and the Reactions.) In need of an immediate replacement, the members of Razz asked Tommy Keene to join the band.[27] As a result, Keene left the Rage and joined Razz.

(After Keene left the Rage, the band dissolved. Richard X. Heyman has gone on to make several excellent albums and EPs as a solo artist: *Actual Size* (1986), *Living Room!!* (1988/90), *Hey Man!* (1991), *Cornerstone* (1998), *Heyman Hoosier & Herman* (2000), *Basic Glee* (2002), and *Rightovers* (2002) [www.richardxheyman.com]. Ricky Street joined the power pop band the Sorrows, who released two highly-regarded albums, *Teenage Heartbreak* (1980) and *Love Too Late* (1981). Jim Dougherty became a member of the rockabilly/roots-rock band Evan Johns and the H-Bombs and played on their classic *Rollin' Through the Night* (1986) album.)

It was in Razz that Keene began to concentrate seriously on songwriting, working in collaboration with Michael Reidy. "I replaced one guitar player who wrote all the music so that's when I first started having to write songs," Keene explained.[28]

With Keene installed on guitar, Razz continued to expand its audience and establish itself as the D.C-area band most likely to succeed. On November 3, 1978, Razz opened for Rockpile at the Student Union Grand Ballroom at the University of Maryland in College Park.[29] The show was broadcast on local FM rock station WHFS. The following year, four songs from the show were released on an EP under the title *Air Time* on the O'Rourke label. The EP included two Keene—Reidy originals, "Marianne" and "Love Is Love," a Behram—Reidy original, "Cherry Vanilla," and a cover of the Chan Romero/Swinging Bluejeans number, "Hippy Hippy Shake." The EP shows that the band had a hard-edged, punkish sound with an aggressive guitar attack. "Love Is Love," with its catchy refrain, is the song that most resembles Keene's later solo work.

In May 1979, Razz released another single, "You Can Run" b/w "Who's Mr. Comedy," on the O'Rourke label.[30]

Razz appeared to be on the verge of breaking through to national success, but the record deal that they were seeking remained elusive, and the frustration of failing to obtain a record deal eventually caused the band to break up. "We kept going to New York doing these showcases, and something wasn't right, something wasn't working, so we disbanded," Keene explained.[31] The band played its final gig on December 27, 1979 at Beacon's Backstage in Falls Church, Virginia.[32]

Following the breakup of Razz, Keene obtained a gig backing new wave pop singer Suzanne Fellini. Fellini released a self-titled album on the Casablanca label in 1980, and scored a minor hit with the song "Love on the Phone." "Richard Heyman called me about backing up Suzanne Fellini—me on guitar and him on drums; she had that song 'Love on the Phone,' kind of Blondie meets Pat Benator—for a six week European tour," Keene recalled. "So I got the job and he didn't. They put me up at the Gramercy Park Hotel. This is really exciting—I'm in New York—and a little frightening because I didn't know anybody. The music wasn't really my scene, but hey, I'm making money and I'm traveling."[33]

(The other members of Razz also remained active in the music scene after the group disbanded. Michael Reidy started a group called MWWW.[34] Bill Craig, Ted Niceley, and Doug Tull teamed up with guitarist and vocalist Michael Colburn to form the band Nightman. Colburn was a veteran of several D.C.-area bands, including a brief stint in Razz in 1972.[35] In 1981, the group released an album entitled *No Escape* on the local Limp label.

Since 1991, Michael Reidy, Abaad Behram, Bill Craig, and Doug Tull have participated in several Razz reunion shows, augmented by various additional musicians.[36] In 2006, Reidy, Behram, Tull, and bassist Greg Shoenborn formed a new group called the Howling Mad. [www.thehowlingmad.com])

When his gig with Suzanne Fellini ended, Keene remained in New York, auditioned for various bands, and ended up forming a band called the Pieces. "I went to Hurrah one night to see this band called the Urban Verbs and I met a guy named Matt [Lambert]," Keene remembered. "We wound up forming a group called Pieces, which meant I stayed in New York for another year"[37] In addition to Keene and Lambert, the group included Kenny Aaronson on bass and Frankie LaRocka on drums.[38]

Keene's role in the Pieces was primarily that of guitarist and backup vocalist. "Once again, there was a main songwriter, and I think I did about two songs," Keene explained. "I mean, I was sort of the guy who sang a song in the set. And, you know, I was a guitar player, backup vocalist."[39]

The Pieces recorded a four-song demo at A&R Studios in New York and played several showcases for record labels, but disbanded when they were unable to obtain a satisfactory record deal.[40] "I mean that group was basically … my heart wasn't in it, I was just trying to … I was hanging out in New York, and I was sleeping on people's couches, and I was trying to think, 'Well, is this going anywhere, I'll just sort of hang around and see if something happens,'" Keene recalled. "And nothing did, so that's when I moved back to D.C. and started my own group."[41]

The Tommy Keene Group

Back in the D.C. area, Keene recruited Razz's former rhythm section of bassist Ted Niceley and drummer Doug Tull to serve as the rhythm section of his new group. Keene also recruited Michael Colburn, who had been playing with Niceley and Tull in Nightman, to play second guitar. Colburn subsequently left the Tommy Keene Group and was replaced by Billy Connelly, who had played with Billy and the Shakes.[42]

In the late summer of 1981, Keene and his band began gigging at venues in the D.C. area such as Desperado's, the Bayou, the 9:30 Club, and the Psychedelly as well as making out-of-town forays to Baltimore and New York. They also began recording demos. Two songs by the group, "Strange Alliance" and "The Heart (Is a Lonely Place to Hide)," were included on *Connected*, a sampler album of acts from the D.C. area that was compiled by Skip Groff of Yesterday and Today Records in Rockville, Maryland and released on his Limp label in October 1981. The two songs that Keene contributed to the album were both strong efforts. "Strange Alliance" is an outstanding piece of guitar-based pop rock, featuring a hard-driving beat, ringing guitar, and an anthemic refrain. "The Heart (Is a Lonely Place to Hide)" is also a catchy pop-rock number, with a melodic piano solo in the middle and an explosive guitar solo at the end.

As a result of his appearance on the *Connected* album, Keene began to receive some favorable press coverage. In his review of *Connected* for *The Washington Post*, Richard Harrington cited Keene's contributions as highlights of the album. "Of all the acts on the sampler, Keene offers the most promise," Harrington wrote. "He has an attractive power-pop sensibility and a fondness for jangly and compelling guitar lines. It makes for a lean, driving, passionate sound that's an effective assimilation of the '60s rock tradition that runs from the Byrds through Tom Petty. 'Strange Alliance' and 'The Heart (Is a Lonely Place to Hide)' stand out on an album that suffers from a slim diet of inspiration. The former features a restlessly innovative melodic structure while the latter has some wonderfully wide-open chords and a tense ambiance that grabs a listener and refuses to let go."[43]

July of the following year saw the release of Keene's first album, *Strange Alliance*, on his own Avenue label.[44] The album contains eight of the demos that Keene and his band had recorded. The demos were produced by Keene and Ted Niceley and recorded at Track Recorders in Silver Spring, Maryland.[45] "I came back from New York and started doing all these demo tapes and a local radio station, WHFS, began playing them," Keene explained. "They were receiving all these requests for the demos, so we pressed them up on vinyl."[46]

Strange Alliance is filled with lots of outstanding guitar-based, pop-rock numbers. The title track, "Landscape," "I Can't See You Anymore," "It's All Happing Today," and "Another Night at Home" all combine catchy pop melodies with hard-driving rhythms and ringing guitar. "All the Way Around" sets a catchy melody to a slow-burning groove, while "Northern Lights" is an atmospheric ballad with spacey slide guitar.

The release of *Strange Alliance* resulted in more positive press coverage for Keene. Joe Sasfy gave the album a favorable review in *The Washington Post*. "Tommy Keene's *Strange Alliance* is full of the conventions of mainstream power pop—the solid hard-rock dynamics of bassist Ted Niceley and drummer Doug Tull, and Keene's memorable melodic tricks and shimmering guitar parts," Sasfy wrote. "Fortunately, Keene has created an impressive musical identity for himself by giving his songs an atmosphere of distressed and soured romanticism that cuts him apart from the legions of power popsters still trading in Tin Pan Alley sentiments. In fact, the disconsolate air that hangs over these songs, Keene's ringing dulcet guitar tones and his whining nasal vocals are all reminiscent of Alex Chilton's brilliantly forlorn Big Star ... Despite their obtuse lyrics and mid-tempo rhythmic rut, all of Keene's songs eventually take hold through some compelling chorus in vibrant instrumental passages."[47]

Writing in Baltimore's *City Paper*, Michael Yockel also praised the album. "Indisputably BaltWash's premier pop rocker, Tommy Keene is poised to jump from regional whiz kid to national phenom, and this eight-song indie could give him the necessary push," Yockel wrote. "Keene writes vibrant love-pop tunes a la the Romantics and 20/20, songs buoyed by his ringing guitar and the middleweight champeen rhythm section of Ted Niceley and Doug Tull. His songs have sufficient edge so that they don't immediately evaporate."[48]

The liner notes for *Strange Alliance* were written by WHFS disc jockey David Einstein. The airplay that Keene received from WHFS during the eighties played an important role in helping to establish him as an artist in the Baltimore/D.C. area. WHFS, which originally was based in Bethesda, Maryland, had begun scheduling progressive rock programming in 1968.[49] The station continued to expand its progressive rock programming during the next few years, and eventually went to an all-progressive rock format around August 1971.[50] During the seventies, WHFS helped to establish the careers of numerous artists, including Bruce Springsteen.[51] By the early eighties, WHFS was one of the few commercial, free-form rock stations left in the country.[52] In the fall of 1983, WHFS relocated to Annapolis, Maryland, which extended its broadcast reach to the Baltimore area. WHFS's ability to survive as a free-form rock station was due in large part to station manager and part-owner Jake Einstein, a long-time radio industry maverick. Under Einstein's leadership, WHFS bucked industry trends toward restricted playlists and heavy rotation of the hits. One of the hallmarks of WHFS was its strong support for local music, and Keene, along with numerous other artists, benefitted greatly from this.

In January 1983, Keene further established his reputation with the release of a single, "Back to Zero Now" b/w "Mr. Roland" on his Avenue label.[53] The A-side features abstract, esoteric lyrics set to a catchy pop melody and framed by acoustic 12-string guitar. This song went on to become one of Keene's most popular numbers. The B-side is a catchy, hard-edge rocker.

The Dolphin Era

Following the release of "Back to Zero Now," Keene obtained a record deal with Dolphin Records, an independent label that was based in Durham, North Carolina and owned by the Record Bar, a chain of record stores located in the South.[54] "They had put out a couple of local bands that I guess hadn't sold well and they told the guy, 'Go out and find more of a regional act that has a following,' and we were playing around D.C., Baltimore and New York at the time and I had a following ..." Keene stated. "Anyway, they had a bit of money behind them because there was this chain of record stores and it was their label."[55]

In April 1984, Dolphin released a six-song EP by Keene entitled *Places That Are Gone*.[56] The EP was produced by Keene and Ted Niceley and recorded at Hit and Run Studios in Rockville, Maryland.[57] Although the band had recorded more than enough material for an album, Dolphin chose the EP format as a good way of introducing a new artist to the public.[58]

The EP opens with an aural montage that segues into the title track. The montage contains the opening part of Richard Rodgers theme from *Victory at Sea*, some dialogue from *101 Dalmatians*, part of the radio broadcast of the 1951 National League pennant playoff game between the Brooklyn Dodgers and the New York Giants, and an excerpt from a Franklin Roosevelt speech to Congress. Keene has stated that the material for the montage was drawn primarily from his parents' record collection, and that it was done as an experiment and does not have any relationship to the title song.[59]

The montage fades out as the opening guitar riff of "Places That Are Gone" comes on. From the opening guitar riff to the anthemic chorus, this song is a pop rock masterpiece and remains one of Keene's most popular songs. It is followed on side one by "Nothing Happened Yesterday," another catchy rocker, and "Baby Face," a melodic ballad backed by acoustic 12-string guitar. Side two opens with "Back to Zero Now," which is followed by "When the Truth Is Found," another strong, upbeat rocker. The EP closes with an exuberant cover of Alex Chilton's "Hey! Little Child."

The EP was very well received. "No District rock artist is more deserving of national attention than Tommy Keene," Joe Sasfy wrote in his review of the EP for *The Washington Post*. "Keene's new, six-song EP, *Places That Are Gone*, restates the virtues of his emotionally skewered power-pop in even more sparkling terms than his earlier *Strange Alliance* EP."[60] Writing in Baltimore's *City Paper*, Michael Yockel gave the EP a rave review. "With his latest record, the six-song mini-LP *Places That Are Gone* (Dolphin), Keene rectifies his earlier vocal shortcomings while solidifying his status as one of the last great guitar tunesmiths," Yockel wrote. "*Places That Are Gone* is crammed with ringing guitars and soaring melodies, plus it's undercut with a plaintive romanticism that shatters existing power pop verities … *Places That Are Gone* is the best guitar pop/rock that I've heard since the Flamin' Groovies' magnificent *Shake Some Action* (1976). Maybe that's partly a function of being a mini-LP, but every song is unremittingly great. Nothing is stretched beyond its limitations. Everything fits. The title cut features layer upon layer of gorgeous rippling guitars that coalesce to intimate a timeless quality that jibes perfectly with the song's lyrical sentiment—that is, a lingering wistfulness for things past that are probably better left untouched … *Places That Are Gone* is a vital, expressive, exquisitely-produced hunk of pop 'n' roll—the most potent release to date by a BaltWash artist."[61]

The release of *Places That Are Gone* brought increased attention to Keene. On June 3, 1984, *The Washington Post* ran a large article about Keene entitled "The Big Breakout" on the front page of its Sunday *Show* section.[62] Also during June, Keene co-headlined a concert (with the Baltimore-based band the Ravyns) at Merriweather Post Pavilion in Columbia, Maryland, a large outdoor venue normally headlined by national acts.

Places That Are Gone eventually went on to bring nation-wide attention to Keene. It was voted best EP of the year in *The Village Voice*'s year-end critics' poll, and it received a four-star review from Parke Puterbaugh in the February 28, 1985 issue of *Rolling Stone*.[63]

The next step was for Keene to record a full-length album for Dolphin Records. Dolphin recruited T-Bone Burnett and Don Dixon to produce the album. "[T]hey said, 'Let's go to the studio and make a full-length record and we'll get a name producer," Keene stated. "So they got two, T-Bone Burnett and Don Dixon …"[64] Burnett and Dixon were both hot producers at the time, Burnett for his work with Los Lobos and Dixon for his work with REM. The album, which was to be titled *Songs from the Film* after a phrase that appeared on the British version of the Beatles' *Help!* and *A Hard Day's Night* albums, was recorded at Reflection Studios in Charlotte, North Carolina in August 1984.[65] The songs recorded for the album were "Back Again," "I Don't Feel Right at All," "Gold Town," "Call on Me," "The Story Ends," "We're Two," "They're in Their Own World," "Run Now," "Faith in Love," "Away from It All," and "Fall Down Too."[66]

In December 1984, "Back Again (Try …)," a song from the upcoming album, was released as a 12-inch single.[67] The song, with its irresistably catchy refrain, is another pop-rock masterpiece. The flip side of the single contains a gorgeous ballad, "Safe in the Light," and live covers of Roxy Music's "All I Need Is You" and the Rolling Stones' "When the Whip Comes Down," which were recorded at the Rat in Boston on July 6, 1984.[68] The single served to maintain Keene's public profile between albums and create interest in the upcoming *Songs from the Film* album.

The Geffen Era

Before *Songs from the Film* could be released by Dolphin, Keene was offered a deal by a major label, Geffen Records.[69] Geffen, however, was not happy with the already-recorded album.[70] "In the interim this A&R guy representing Geffen saw us and said 'I want to sign you,' and I said 'Well, I have this record coming out on Dolphin'—we'd finished it, but we hadn't mixed it—and I gave him a tape and he took it back and played it and they hated it!," Keene stated. "And they said, 'If you put this out, the deal's off.' We'd been trying to get a record deal for about three and a half years, which may not sound like a very long time, but when you're 21 or 22 it's an eternity. We'd had a lot of people sniffing around, but no one else was offering us a record deal. So we went for it, and we said to Dolphin, 'We're gonna do this deal with Geffen.' But they had this album in the can that they'd spent a lot of money on. They managed to work out a deal, Dolphin and Geffen, where Dolphin got money from *Songs from the Film*'s royalties."[71]

Once Keene was signed to Geffen, a producer had to be selected to oversee the recording of the new version of *Songs from the Film*. "The record company and I couldn't agree on who to use," Keene stated. "I wanted to use Bob Clearmountain. I wanted to go in there with a really good engineer. And they said, 'No, we want to go into the studio for your first record with more of a producer-type who can flesh out your songs a little bit.'"[72] The producer eventually agreed on was Geoff Emerick, best known as an engineer for the Beatles and the producer of Badfinger's *No Dice* album and Elvis Costello's *Imperial Bedroom* album.

Keene and his band recorded the new version of *Songs from the Film* with Emerick at AIR Studios on the island of Montserrat in the West Indies.[73] When the album was finished, however, Keene was not entirely happy with it. Keene felt that the album was too laid-back and soft sounding, and failed to capture the band's live sound.[74] "A lot of the songs worked really great with Geoff Emerick's production style, like 'The Story Ends,'" Keene stated. "But we all wanted to make a new record that would come close to our live sound. We came out with this really nice, textured, sort of laid-back record and everybody was going 'uh-oh.'"[75]

"We'd hired Geoff Emerick as the producer because he had worked with the Beatles, but I don't think he had listened to the radio in 20 years," Keene further stated. "In the '80s to get radio airplay you needed a 'big' drum sound and Emerick hated that. The drums on the record ended up sounding tiny."[76]

To try to salvage things, the album's scheduled release date of October 1985 was postponed and several of the album's tracks were remixed by Bill Wittman at the Record Plant in New York City to try to give them a tougher sound.[77] Wittman had been associate producer and engineer on Cyndi Lauper's *She's So Unusual* album and had produced Graham Parker's *Steady Nerves* album. Four of the tracks that were remixed by Wittman were used on the final album.[78]

Songs from the Film was finally released in February 1986. The album contains a remake of "Places That Are Gone," ten new Keene originals, and a cover of Lou Reed's "Kill Your Sons."

Unlike past releases, which had received mainly excellent notices, *Songs from the Film* received something of a mixed reaction from critics and fans. Much of the criticism centered on the album's production. Some people felt that, in the move to a major label, Keene's sound had been watered down. I remember hearing a disc jockey on a local college radio station describe the record as sounding as if it had "had all of the energy taken out of it." Writing in *The Washington Post*, Joe Sasfy stated that "[w]hile *Songs from the Film* reasserts the pleasing pop craft displayed on those earlier EPs, it is not the impressive leap forward in sound or creative expression some fans may have hoped for."[79] Also writing in *The Washington Post*, Geoffrey Himes stated that Emerick had "proceeded to enervate and stifle everything that was likable about Keene."[80] Michael Yockel voiced similar sentiments in Baltimore's *City Paper*, describing the album as "high gloss, beautifully crafted, and excrutiatingly dull."[81]

On the other hand, some people felt that the album's production was an improvement over past efforts. Writing in the *Baltimore Sun*, J.D. Considine stated that "the sound of the album, with its beefy guitars and punchy mix, is a quantum leap from the thin sound of his EPs, coming closer to Mr. Keene's concert sound."[82] In his review of the album for *Rolling Stone*, Rob Tannenbaum stated that "it's possible to hear the records as a refreshing return to the pretechnocratic days when hit singles resulted from ingenuous, penetrating hooks rather than flagrant studio production."[83]

Coming on the heels of two masterpieces, *Places That Are Gone* and "Back Again (Try …)," expectations were high and perhaps it was inevitable that there would be some disappointment with the album. Also, criticism of the album was probably fueled in part by a backlash that occurred against Keene, particularly in certain quarters of the D.C. press and music scene, engendered by resentment of his success. (This reached its peak later in the year with D.C.'s *City Paper* naming *Songs from the Film* the year's "biggest flop.") In retrospect, *Songs from the Film* holds up very well. For the most part, Geoff Emerick's production is an asset, allowing the band to achieve a far broader range of sounds and textures than they had done in the past, without any really significant loss of energy. And the album contains some of Keene's finest songs. "My Mother Looked Like Marilyn Monroe" and "Underworld" are both classics. "In Our Lives," "Listen to Me," and "As Life Goes By" are catchy pop-rock numbers; "Astronomy," "Gold Town," and "Paper Words and Lies" are sharp-edged rockers; and "The Story Ends" is a lovely ballad. The hard-rocking cover of "Kill Your Sons" is another standout track and actually much better than the rather bland original version on Lou Reed's *Sally Can't Dance* album.

The remake of "Places That Are Gone" was slated as the first single from the album, but its release in the U.S. was delayed and then scrapped due to the independent promoters scandal, which had just broken.[84] "The song was never able to break at Top 40 radio … because at the time there was a payola scandal going on in the industry and Geffen's radio promo guy didn't want to have to pay anybody to play the record or even be associated with that scene," Keene explained.[85] As a result, the single was released only in Canada. The single features a non-LP song, "Faith in Love," on the flipside. This is an acoustic ballad produced by Keene and recorded at Hit and Run.[86] A video for "Places That Are Gone" also was produced and received airplay on MTV.[87] Later in the year, "Listen to Me" was released as a single in the U.S., also with "Faith in Love" on the flipside.

Keene and his band undertook a 20-date tour in support of *Songs from the Film*, which took them to the Midwest and West Coast for the first time. Drummer Doug Tull threw his back out before the start of the tour and was temporarily replaced for the tour by Rob Brill.[88] The tour included a series of dates opening for Lloyd Cole and the Commotions. One of these, at the World in New York City on March 21, was filmed and broadcast on MTV.

Songs from the Film ultimately failed to provide Keene with a major commercial breakthrough. The album entered the *Billboard* album chart on March 29 and spent 17 weeks on the chart, peaking at number 148.[89] While this was a perfectly respectable showing for an album by a new artist, it was somewhat short of the expectations of a major label like Geffen.

Over the summer, Keene appeared with a song called "Run Now" on the soundtrack of *Out of Bounds*, a movie starring Anthony Michael Hall. The song was produced by Bob Clearmountain and recorded at Bearsville Studios in Bearsville, New York in January 1986.[90] Keene and his band also made a cameo appearance in the movie, performing "Run Now" during a nightclub scene. "Geffen was going to do the soundtrack, and there were parts for two bands in the film," Keene explained. "They already had Siouxsie and the Banshees, and they wanted someone else. The two people it came down to were me and Chris Isaak. So we sent them a demo of the song 'Run Now,' and the director really liked it because it fit the part of the movie where Anthony Michael Hall was being chased through a club. So, somehow, I ended up getting the gig over Chris Isaak. I was on the set for two long days. Anthony Michael Hall actually brushes past me in the scene, and I jump out of the way. That was my acting debut—overacting, I should say."[91]

The band, with Doug Tull back in the drum seat, also gigged around the East Coast occasionally during the summer.

In October 1986, Geffen released a six-song EP by Keene entitled *Run Now*. In addition to the title track, the EP includes a remix of "Back Again," three additional songs from the T-Bone Burnett/Don Dixon sessions for *Songs from the Film*, and a live version of "Kill Your Sons" from the World gig. The EP was intended to maintain Keene's visibility until his next full-length record could be released, and to try to win back fans who were disappointed in *Songs from the Film* and interested in hearing material from the T-Bone Burnett/Don Dixon sessions.[92]

Unfortunately, the EP is not among Keene's better records. "Run Now" is a reasonably catchy rocker, but suffers from Bob Clearmountain's bombastic production. (The version of "Run Now" that appears on the EP has a longer guitar outro than the version that appears on the *Out of Bounds* soundtrack album.[93]) "Back Again" sounds as great as ever, but the remix is virtually indistinguishable from the original mix. The other songs from the T-Bone Burnett/Don Dixon sessions are all nice enough but largely unexceptional. The one standout track is the live version of "Kill Your Sons." The track showcases Keene's electrifying guitar playing and demonstrates the energy and excitement that the band was capable of generating onstage.

Keene and his band undertook a 25-date tour in support of the *Run Now* EP, starting on November 1 and concluding on December 16.

The press release that accompanied *Run Now* stated that "a new record is planned for late spring/early summer."[94] Similarly, in an interview at the time that *Run Now* was released, Keene stated that "We're looking to start recording in March or April, and should probably have the album out in late July or August."[95] As it turned out, however, it would be considerably longer before Keene's next album actually appeared. Geffen was losing interest in Keene and was reluctant to allow him to record another album. "It was at this point that Geffen started to lose interest too," Keene said. "They wouldn't let me record another record for two and a half years although they eventually had to because it was in my contract."[96]

While work on a new record was being delayed, Keene's band was breaking up. Doug Tull left the band in December 1986, after the tour in support of the *Run Now* EP.[97] The band played some gigs in the spring of 1987 with a new drummer and, after that, Billy Connelly and Ted Niceley also departed. During the remainder of 1987, Keene gigged as a solo act, opening shows for artists such as Alex Chilton, Marti Jones and Don Dixon, and Suzanne Vega.

(After leaving the Tommy Keene Group, Billy Connelly—now billed as Will Connelly—pursued a solo career, with Doug Tull playing drums in his band. The It's About Music label has released an album of recordings made by Connelly from 1989 to 1992 under the title *Whisper to Me*, as well as another album by Connelly entitled *Assumption*. [www.itsaboutmusic.com] Ted Nicely has remained active as a producer, producing recordings for Fugazi, the Dead Milkmen, Jawbox, and Girls Against Boys among others. As noted earlier, Doug Tull is currently playing drums with his former Razz bandmates Michael Reidy and Abaad Behram in the Howling Mad. [www.thehowlingmad.com])

Keene spent 1988 largely out of the public spotlight, during which time he relocated to California.[98] During the summer of 1988, he finally recorded his next album, *Based on Happy Times*. The new album was recorded at Ardent Studios in Memphis and produced by Keene, John Hampton, and Joe Hardy.[99] Hampton and Hardy had served as engineers on various Alex Chilton projects as well as the Replacements' *Pleased to Meet Me* album. In addition to producing, Hampton played drums and Hardy played bass on the new album. After finishing work on the album, Keene completed his college degree in sociology from the

University of Maryland, earning his last credits at UCLA during its fall sem-ster.[100]

Based on Happy Times was released in February 1989. In contrast with *Songs from the Film*, *Based on Happy Times* features stripped-down arrangements and a hard-edged guitar sound that more closely reflects Keene's live sound. The album contains hard-edged rockers with buoyant melodies such as "Nothing Can Change You," "Light of Love," "This Could Be Fiction," "Highwire Days," and "Hanging onto Yesterday," as well as brooding ballads like "The Biggest Con-flict" and the title track. The album also contains two songs that Keene co-wrote with Jules Shear, "When Our Vows Break" and "If We Run Away," both of which are catchy pop-rock numbers. In addition, the album contains a raucous, blues-rock cover of the Beach Boys' "Our Car Club," which Keene had originally played with Razz.[101] The CD version of the album contains a bonus track, "Where Have All Your Friends Gone," which was not included on the vinyl or cassette versions of the album. The album closes with a somber ballad about sui-cide, "A Way Out."

Based on Happy Times received favorable reviews and was generally viewed as a return to form following *Songs from the Film*. "... longtime Bethesda hope Tommy Keene has made an auspicious return of sorts, infusing his recently released *Based on Happy Times* (Geffen) with much of the energy and punch sorely lacking in 1986's *Songs from the Film*, an album that showed him at a pro-fessional crisis point," Michael Anft wrote in the Baltimore *Evening Sun*. "Keene's strength has always been his ability to weave vignettes of life and love around his tough signature guitar playing ... He returns to the best formula here with a bang on the likes of 'Nothing Can Change You' and 'Light of Love,' as well as the R.E.M.-ish 'Pictures.' Although the two collaborations with Jules Shear are too shallow and empty to score a hit, it's nice to see that Tommy's back on the right track again, even if he's not quite back to zero."[102] Writing in *Rolling Stone*, Moira McCormick stated, "Keene's inexhaustable supply of engaging mel-odies and indelible hooks is matched by an ability to string them together in novel ways ... Nobody casts as jaundiced an eye on romance and sets it to such mercilessly catchy melodies as Tommy Keene ..."[103]

In late March, Keene embarked on a tour in support of the album, including a series of dates opening for the Replacements. Keene's new band featured Justin Hibbard on guitar, Brad Quinn (formerly of Carnival Season) on bass, and John Richardson on drums. The concerts showcased material from the new album as well as debuting some not-yet-released songs such as "Alive," "Hey Man," and "No One in This City."

After a year's absence it was great to see Keene back in action. Unfortunately, the writing was on the wall with respect to Keene's relationship with Geffen, and the record label dropped Keene from its roster not long after the release of *Based on Happy Times*.[104] Keene received the news while on tour in support of the album.[105] "My management called me up and said, 'You've been dropped by Geffen, your booking agency has canceled the rest of the tour, and we aren't going to work with you either,'" he recalled. "That was quite a day."[106] With little support from the record company, *Based on Happy Times* did not stand much chance of success, and the album failed to chart.[107]

Keene continued to gig in the summer of 1989 and, with Eric Peterson (formerly of the dBs) replacing Justin Hibbard on guitar, in 1990 and 1991. At these shows Keene continued to debut strong new material such as "Compromise," "Crack City," "Down, Down, Down," and "Love Is a Dangerous Thing." Keene also recorded demos of new material at Hit and Run Studios to shop around to record labels. While he received some interest from major labels, another record deal with a major label remained elusive.[108]

Also during 1991, Keene, Brad Quinn, and John Richardson toured as the backing band for Adam Schmitt, who was touring in support of his debut album, *World So Bright*.[109] Keene, Quinn, and Richardson, as well as Jay Bennett, all appeared on Schmitt's follow-up album, *Illiterature*, which was released in 1993.[110]

The Matador Era

Unable to score a deal with a major label, Keene released a five-song EP, *Sleeping on a Rollercoaster*, on the independent Matador label in September 1992. The five songs were drawn from the Hit and Run sessions, with four of them remixed by John Hampton at Ardent Studios. The EP is fantastic and probably Keene's best work since *Places That Are Gone* and "Back Again (Try …)." The EP opens with the hard-edged, punkish rocker "Love Is a Dangerous Thing." This is followed by "Driving into the Sun," a catchy pop-rock number. Next up is "Down, Down, Down," a sad, yearning ballad set to martial-like drum rolls and powerful guitar chords. This is followed by "Alive," an ultra-catchy and highly propulsive rocker that had long been a highlight of Keene's live shows. The EP closes with the beautiful, lyrical ballad, "Waiting to Fly." The strong quality of the EP suggested that perhaps Keene does his best work without the participation of an outside producer or interference from a major label.

The EP received very favorable reviews. "Still catchy after all these years," J.D. Considine wrote in *Musician*. "Keene's songwriting remains every bit as sharp as when he was a major-label contender. The best songs here, 'Love Is a Dangerous Thing' and 'Alive' are classic examples of guitar-pop perfection, with rippling Byrds-ian rhythm licks, blissfully harmonized choruses, and irresistibly melancholy minor-key melodies. Somebody get this guy a deal!"[111]

While *Sleeping on a Rollercoaster* received positive reviews, it failed to create the sort of buzz generated by some of Keene's earlier releases. By this point, Keene's career had lost much of the momentum that it had gained in the mid-eighties. Given Keene's age at this time and the rising popularity of "alternative" and "grunge" music, the chances of him landing another major label deal were becoming less likely.

Keene's career was dealt a further blow around this time by the loss of support from WHFS. In January 1988, Jake Einstein and the other owners of WHFS sold the station to Duchossois Communications of Elmhurst, Illinois.[112] Although the terms of the deal required Duchossois to retain WHFS' progressive rock format, Duchossois gradually made changes to the station's format and most of its best disc jockeys soon departed.[113] By the early nineties, WHFS had jumped on the "alternative" bandwagon and stopped giving airplay to Keene and many other acts that it had previously supported. "My audience dropped at least 75% when they stopped playing me, around the *Sleeping* EP, circa 92," Keene stated.[114]

Keene toured in support of the *Sleeping on a Rollercoaster* EP in the fall of 1992 and, with Jay Bennett (of Wilco) replacing Eric Peterson on guitar, toured again in early 1993.

In August 1993, Keene released a compilation album, *The Real Underground*, on the independent Alias label. The album contains the entire *Places That Are Gone* EP, outtakes/demos from the mid-eighties, "Back Again" and "Safe in the Light" from the 12" single, "Mr. Roland" from the flipside of the "Back to Zero Now" single, and demos recorded at Hit and Run Studios between 1989 and 1991. The album is not a comprehensive retrospective since it does not contain any material from *Strange Alliance*, any of the Geffen releases, or the *Sleeping on a Rollercoaster* EP. It does an excellent job, however, of pulling together on CD all of Keene's mid-eighties work as well as providing lots of great, previously-unreleased tracks. The outtakes from the *Places That Are Gone* era such as "Something Got a Hold on Me" and "That You Do" hold their own with the tracks that were actually issued on the EP. And the demos from 1989 to 1991 are full of great songs like the ultra-catchy "Hey Man" and "Something to Rave About" and the cover of the Flamin' Groovies' "Shake Some Action," which Keene often used as an encore number.

Also in 1993, Keene contributed a song called "Disarray" to a pop compilation album called *Yellow Pills, The Best of American Pop, vol. 1* compiled by Jordan Oakes of the *Yellow Pills* zine.

On February 1, 1994, Keene and his band kicked off a tour in support of *The Real Underground* with an appearance on *The Late Show with Conan O'Brien*. They performed "Places That Are Gone" and Keene chatted briefly with O'Brien.

From October 1994 to March 1995 Keene toured as a guitarist with Velvet Crush, who were touring in support of their *Teenage Symphonies to God* album.[115] Keene can be heard playing with Velvet Crush on the live *Rock Concert* EP, which was recorded at the Cabaret Metro in Chicago in March 1995. Also in 1995, Keene contributed a cover of "Carrie Anne" to a Hollies tribute album entitled *sing HOLLIES in reverse*.

February 1996 saw the release of *Ten Years After*, Keene's first full-length album for the Matador label. Keene was backed on the album by Brad Quinn on bass and vocals and John Richardson on drums and percussion, with additional musicians appearing on various tracks.[116] The album was recorded and mixed partly by Steve Carr at Hit and Run Studios and partly by Adam Schmitt at Private Studios in Urbana, Illinois and at Pachyderm in Cannon Falls, Minnesota.[117]

"I named it *Ten Years After* because it was an in-joke because the first Geffen album, *Songs from the Film* had been released 10 years before on the same day," Keene said in explanation of the album's enigmatic title. "I also like the band Ten Years After and thought it was a cool title having to do with longevity."[118]

Ten Years After was another outstanding effort from Keene. With this album Keene came closer than ever before to capturing his live sound, backing his catchy pop melodies and melancholy lyrics with loud, distorted guitars and explosive drumming. One of the standout tracks on the album is "Compromise," which had been a highlight of Keene's live shows for years. Powered by an irresistibly catchy and propulsive guitar riff and John Richardson's powerhouse drumming, this is a pop-rock masterpiece. The album contains plenty of other catchy, sharp-edged rockers such as "Going Out Again," "Today and Tomorrow," and "On the Runway." There also are strong melodic ballads such as "Your Heart Beats Alone" and "Good Thing Going." The album also found Keene expanding his musical palette and incorporating some country influences into his sound for the first time. The largely-acoustic "If You're Getting Married Tonight" features a weeping pedal steel guitar played by Eric Heywood, and the catchy mid-tempo number "You Can't Wait for Time" is reminiscent of the country-rock sounds of the Byrds and Tom Petty. The album closes with the darkly brooding "Before the Lights Go Down." (It is followed on both the CD and LP by an unlisted bonus track, a brief snippet of Pete Townshend's "It's Not True," which Keene had played in concert for years, tacked onto the end of various songs.)

Once again, the album received positive notices from the press. "It isn't just that this is the Washington native's best-sounding album to date, conveying all the sonic might of his stage sound without compromising the charm of his melancholy melodies," J.D. Considine wrote in the Baltimore *Sun*. "The album is a feast of fully cranked guitar and catchy pop choruses. From 'We Started Over,' with its Who-like instrumental interplay and soaring minor-key chorus, to the roaring guitars and heartbreak vocals of 'Turning on Blue,' Keene blends power and passion with practiced ease."[119] Writing in *Audities*, Terry Hermon stated "… it's loud and it's crammed full of melody-driven guitar pop … the guitar playing throughout is the work of a true craftsman."[120]

During the late winter and spring of 1996, Keene toured in support of the *Ten Years After* album as an opening act for the Gin Blossoms. In the summer of

1996, Keene toured as a guitarist for Paul Westerberg, who was touring in support of his *Eventually* album. Later in the year, Keene contributed the song "No One in This City" to a compilation album called *The Bucketfull of Brains 50th Anniversary CD*, which came with issue #50 of the British zine *Bucketfull of Brains*.

In February 1998, Keene's next album, *Isolation Party*, was released by Matador. The songs on the album were performed primarily by a core group that consisted of Keene on vocals and guitar, John Richardson on drums and percussion, and Jay Bennett on bass, organ, and guitar.[121] The core group was augmented by other musicians on various tracks.[122] The album was recorded at Short Order Recorders in Zion, Illinois and Private Studios in Urbana, Illinois.[123]

"Actually Jay Bennett came up with the name," Keene said in explanation of the album's title. "It was kind of a joke in the studio, where you're listening to your weird mix of the record. One track was soloed up. It was me just doing some kind of embellishment, sort of a fussy part, and he said, 'Look, Tommy's having an isolation party.' When you isolate a particular track ... you know, he was just sort of saying that I was kind of going to town. It just became a big joke and then we kept saying it. Then I was searching for an album title and it just seemed to fit ... It just hit me one day when I was sitting there agonizing about what to call the record."[124]

Isolation Party is a particular standout among Keene's albums—from the opening blast of guitar in "Long Time Missing" to the quiet closing notes of "Twilight's in Town," *Isolation Party* is a classic and masterful album. Every track on the album is fantastic, making it the best and most-fully realized album's of Keene's career up to that point. *Isolation Party* features all of the familiar hallmarks of Keene's style: expertly-crafted pop tunes, obliquely introspective and melancholy lyrics, and lots of electrifying guitar playing. At the same time the songs are more stylistically varied and the production shows great strides forward. Although the album remains guitar-oriented, it features a wider variety of sounds and textures, with each song taking on its own distinct personality.

The album's opening track, "Long Time Missing," is a classic pop-rock number, setting a wonderfully catchy melody to an abrasive, insistent guitar riff and a driving beat. "Getting Out from Under You," "The World Outside," and "Battle Lines" are also catchy, sharp-edged rockers. The quietly reflective "Never Really Been Gone" sets a gorgeous melody to a wall of ringing guitar. The acoustic-based "Tuesday Morning" features a jaunty rhythm and uncharacteristically happy-go-lucky air. Another highlight of the album is a killer version of Mission of Burma's "Einstein's Day," which provides an excellent showcase for both

Keene's singing and guitar playing. The album closes with "Weak and Watered Down" and "Twilight's in Town," two of the sort of brooding, melancholy ballads that are a Keene specialty.

The album once again proved a hit with critics. Writing in the British rock magazine *Q*, Peter Kane awarded the album four stars and gave it a rave review. "Blessed with sun kissed melodies and copious amounts of well struck guitar, *Isolation Party* should, by rights, finally see him exchange his cult status for something more tangible," Kane wrote. "It's a tremendous record, unashamedly retro in feel that, much like Matthew Sweet at his peak circa *Girlfriend*, pieces together the best of Big Star, Replacements, Husker Du, and all the usual suspects in fact, yet still manages to make it sound all shiny and new. Recommendations really can't come much higher."[125]

Keene toured in support of the *Isolation Party* album during May of 1998, with Scott Johnson (of the Gin Blossoms) replacing Jay Bennett on guitar. In July 1998, Geffen reissued *Songs from the Film* on CD with nine bonus tracks. During the summer, Keene played a few additional dates in Chicago and the Washington, D.C. area, two of his strongest markets, with Steve Gerlach (formerly of the Phantom Helmsmen) replacing Scott Johnson on guitar.

In late November and early December of 1998, Keene and his band did a two-week residency at the Chesterfield Cafe in Paris. Brad Jones substituted on bass for Brad Quinn during this series of shows. This marked the first time that Keene had played in Europe, other than as a sideman for Suzanne Fellini and Velvet Crush.

"Well, the Paris show was very strange," Keene stated. "It was kind of a touristy, American-style bar, and they like to bring American bands over. If you looked at who had been there, they had a pretty amazing roster of people who had done this two-week residency. Everyone from Alanis Morrisette to the Posies. But the kind of bar that it was, it was really sort of like playing a Thank God It's Friday's or something. It was really kind of a bogus situation. You had people sitting there eating in front of you."[126]

"Paris, as you can imagine, is a pretty esoteric audience to play for, and we were playing in possibly the most un-esoteric place," Keene continued. "That was just sort of a fun thing to go over and do for two weeks. There was a handful of people who would come each night who were familiar with the band. It was just sort of 'Let's go to Paris for two weeks and get paid.'"[127]

Keene and his band made their second foray to Europe in February 2000, when they undertook a 10-date tour of Spain. This proved to be a more positive experience than their residency at the Chesterfield Cafe in Paris.

"Now, Spain was the exact opposite," Keene stated. "In Spain we played clubs, and the people had the records, and they knew the music, and they came, and they were fans."[128]

"Spain was a completely different story," Keene continued. "Spain was a real tour, we played 10 different cities, we did a t.v. show, we did numerous radio interviews on the national radio. And I did an in-store at the big record store in downtown Madrid. I played a solo set the day of the Madrid show I think, or the day after. So that was like doing a tour of Spain. People knew the songs and had the records. It was really quite interesting."[129]

On returning from Spain, Keene and his band played a show in Chicago, and then played a few shows on the East Coast during the early summer.

From *Showtunes* to *Crashing the Ether*

Keene has long been known as a dynamic live performer and, in October 2001, he finally released a live album entitled *Showtunes*. The album was recorded at shows during the spring and summer of 1998 and the summer of 2000. "… in '98, the tour for *Isolation Party*, I think we recorded about 10 [shows]," Keene said. "I listened to all of those. Some of them I didn't even bother to rough mix because they were just bad-sounding rooms, or there was a technical difficulty at a certain club, or something screwed up where the bass didn't record that night. Out of those 10 shows there was one show that was just exceptional. Most of the record is from that night—it's one of the Iota shows. I think 85% of the record is from that one show. It was just a really good night and we caught it."[130]

"So I listened to those shows," Keene continued. "I think there were two songs from Chicago, one song from New York, and the rest was D.C. And then there was one song from a show we did in Lexington, Kentucky where there was about 20 people there. There's a great version of 'Marilyn Monroe' and the rest of the show sounded like crap. So I listened to those, and I thought, 'Well, I don't quite have everything I want.'

"So, the summer of 2000 we did two more shows at Iota and we recorded those. After that, I listened to those, and I said, 'O.k., now I have the record.' Because there was about five songs that I wanted on the record that I did not have good versions of. For example, I remember, 'Long Time Missing,' I didn't have a good version of that. 'Going Out Again,' I didn't have a good one of that.

"So, I'd say … how many songs on the record? Fifteen? There's probably nine from that one night in '98 at Iota, two Chicago, one New York, one Kentucky, and probably three ... that's more than 15 ... three from the 2000 Iota shows."[131]

Showtunes was released by Keene himself through a production and distribution deal with Parasol Records, an independent label based in Champaign, Illinois. "Well, frankly, the '98 record, *Isolation Party*, came out on Matador, and I thought after three records we'd taken that relationship as far as it would go," Keene explained. "I offered it to them, and they really weren't interested in a live record. I find that people just don't care as much about live records as they used to. Which is kind of a drag, because I really like live records. In the seventies and eighties—well, I guess the seventies was really the boon for live records—live records made peoples' careers—Cheap Trick or Humble Pie or J. Giels or Peter Frampton or ... there's a long list of people."[132]

"I think with the advent of MTV, the internet, DVDs, a live record is not as special as it used to be," Keene continued. "... People weren't interested, so I just did it myself and did a P & D deal, which is production and distribution, with this little label out of Champaign called Parasol. They distributed the record, pressed it, and worked the press a little bit."[133]

Showtunes proved to be a really fantastic live album. The 15 songs on the album were selected and sequenced to approximate a fairly typical set. The album is brimming with classic songs, including "Long Time Missing," "Nothing Can Change You," "Underworld," "Going Out Again," "My Mother Looked Like Marilyn Monroe," "Compromise," "Back to Zero Now," and "Places That Are Gone." Unlike a lot of live albums that are extensively doctored in the studio, *Showtunes* accurately reflects the live sound of the band and does an excellent job of capturing the energy and excitement of a live show.

Keene's next studio album, *The Merry-Go-Round Broke Down*, was released on the independent spinART label in June 2002. The album is named after the theme music for the *Looney Toones* cartoons. Keene was backed on the album by Brad Quinn on bass, John Richardson on drums, and Jay Bennett on keyboards, with additional musicians appearing on various tracks.[134] The album was recorded at Mayberry Studio in Tempe, Arizona, Calle de Maria in Palm Springs, California, Private Studios in Urbana, Illinois, and Pieholden Studio in Chicago, Illinois.[135]

As usual, *The Merry-Go-Round Broke Down* delivers lots of great guitar pop, such as "Begin Where We End," "All Your Love Will Stay," and "Time Will Take You Today," as well as melodic and melancholy ballads like "Hanging Over My Head," "The World Where I Still Live," and "Circumstance." At the same time, the album found Keene pushing the boundaries of his pop sound and venturing into new musical territory. The album incorporates some different musical styles, has an increased use of keyboards, and utilizes horns for the first time.

One of the biggest musical departures on the album is "The Man Without a Soul," a bluesy rocker with boogie-woogie piano and a horn section. This number is reminiscent of the Rolling Stones circa *Sticky Fingers*. "I think when I wrote 'The Man Without a Soul' it just screamed for horns a la 'All the Way from Memphis' or some mid-period Stones songs," Keene stated. "It was just sort of fun to do. I thought, finally here's a song I wrote I can put horns on."[136] Also in the blues-rock vein is "The Fog Has Lifted," a heavy-duty rocker backed by walls of guitar distortion.

And then there is the centerpiece of the album—a 16-minute number entitled "The Final Hour." This is not a three-minute song with a long guitar jam tacked onto the end of it—rather it is a carefully constructed mini-rock opera with recurring musical motifs and a narrative story line. Appropriately enough, the song shows a strong Who influence—at times the interplay between Keene's guitar and John Richardson's drums is reminiscent of that between Pete Townshend and Keith Moon.

"Well, I was in the writing process for the record, and I had a lot of ideas that were incomplete songs, or little bits and pieces," Keene said with respect to the origins of "The Final Hour." "And I just got the idea to write a long piece. I thought originally it would be about eight minutes or nine minutes long. Of course I was inspired by … more 'A Quick One While He's Away' from the Who than *Tommy*. I didn't have ambitions on that scale."[137]

"Once again it was an attempt to try something different, where I would have to come up with a narrative and a story," Keene continued. "The piece itself has recurring themes and motifs like an opera does. There's a beginning, a middle, and an end. It was just kind of a challenging thing to do. I was trying to do something different."[138]

Recording such a long piece presented challenges. "We did the first third of the song in one take," Keene explained. "Then we did part two, with the speeded-up tempo, which is about eight minutes … or, about nine minutes actually. We played all the way out to the end, but near the end of the second part when the tempo changes, the engineer tapped the right click track into the drummer's 'phones and he kind of pulls it back. You never hear him do it, but he does a good job of it."[139]

Once again, the album received positive notices from the press. "… *Merry-Go-Round* turns up the amps and rocks unabashedly," Bill Holmes wrote in *Bucket-*

full of Brains. "Possibly Keene's best record ever, and considering his catalogue that's saying a lot."[140]

Keene and his band toured in support of *The Merry-Go-Round Broke Down* in August 2002. During October and November 2002, Keene performed several dates as a solo act. Keene and his band also played a handful of dates in August and September 2003.

June 2004 saw the release of *Drowning: A Tommy Keene Miscellany* on Not Lame, an independent label based in Fort Collins, Colorado. The album is a collection of rarities and previously unreleased material. It contains songs that were previously released on various-artist compilations such as "Disarray," which appeared on *Yellow Pills: The Best of American Pop, volume 1,* "Carrie Anne," which appeared on *sing HOLLIES in reverse,* and "There's No One In This City," which appeared on *The Bucketfull of Brains 50th Anniversary CD*; songs that appeared on non-U.S. releases such as "The Scam and the Flim Flam Man," which appeared on the U.K. version of *Places That Are Gone,* "Tell Me Something," which appeared on the U.K.-only *Driving into the Sun,* and "Soul Searching" and "Karl Marx," which appeared on the Japanese version of *Ten Years After,* and previously-unreleased songs such as "Drowning," "A Wish Ago," and "We'll Always Remain Just the Same."

The fact that these songs did not make it onto an album at the time that they were originally recorded is in no way a reflection of the quality of the songs. The material on *Drowning* is consistently strong throughout the album. Indeed, *Drowning* holds its own with Keene's other albums and contains songs that rank among his finest. The album kicks off with the title track, which exemplifies Keene's approach to guitar pop by combining a heavy guitar sound with a catchy pop tune and melancholy lyrics. The long-time concert favorite, "There's No One in this City," is a classic Tommy Keene track. On "Tell Me Something," Keene adds a bit of funk to his pop sound, with a four-on-the-floor beat and some scratchy guitar. "A Wish Ago" is a fantastic guitar pop number, combining a wonderful melody with chiming guitar. "Watch the World Go By" and "We'll Always Remain Just the Same" are similarly great guitar pop numbers. The piano-based "I Know It's Blue" adds some variety amidst all of the guitars.

During September Keene played a few dates on the East Coast and during November he played a few dates on the West Coast. For these shows, Mike Leach, Keene's soundman, substituted on drums for John Richardson, who was touring with Badfinger. For most of the shows, Keene opened for Guided by Voices, who were on their farewell tour.

For his next album, *Crashing the Ether*, Keene took a different approach, setting up a home studio and recording the album himself.[141] John Richardson played drums and Keene handled most of the other instruments himself, playing guitar, keyboards, harmonica, and bass.[142] The album also features guest appearances on various tracks by members of the Tommy Keene Group as well as other musicians.[143]

"It was really liberating," Keene said about recording at home. "I'd always thought that the more people I brought into a solo album the more 'personality' it would have. This time, I tried the Prince routine, and it was just a freeing experience. Every night, I could go and practice in my home studio and overdub any instrument until I got it right."[144]

At the same time that Keene was recording *Crashing the Ether* he also was working on a recording project in collaboration with Guided by Voices frontman Robert Pollard. "A few years ago a writer friend of mine [Matt Hickey] was interviewing Bob and brought my name up ... and he'd mentioned that he liked my music," Keene explained. "My friend asked, 'Would you like to work with him?' And Bob said, "Yeah, I would."[145]

This resulted in plans for Keene and Pollard to collaborate on an album. Keene explained their approach to the album: "We talked a little bit about direction; he is a fan of mine and he said, 'I want a Tommy Keene record and I want to do my thing to it. You write the music, send it to me; I'll write the lyrics and I'll sing over what you give me.'"[146]

Keene recorded the instrumental tracks for the collaborative album in his home studio, playing most of the instruments himself.[147] John Richardson and Jon Wurster (of Superchunk and the Robert Pollard band) contributed drums.[148] Keene sent the completed instrumental tracks to Pollard, who wrote lyrics and melodies for the tracks, and added his vocals to them.[149]

The two recording projects on which Keene had been working both came to fruition in 2006, which proved to be a particularly eventful year. The year started with Keene playing guitar and keyboards in Robert Pollard's post-Guided by Voices touring band. While opening shows for GBV on their farewell tour, Keene had offered his services as a guitarist to Pollard for his next tour. "... I went up to him in San Francisco and said, 'I don't want to steal someone else's gig, but if you need a guitarist for your next tour, I'd love to do it,'" Keene explained. "He said, 'Can you do it? That sounds great!'"[150] The tour, in support of Pollard's first post-GBV solo album *From a Compound Eye*, ran from January through April.

In April, Keene's *Crashing the Ether* album was released by the Eleven Thirty label, a subsidiary of the North Carolina-based Yep Roc label. With respect to the album's title, Keene explained," ... I was reading a book of 30s to 60s hipster slang and the phrase 'crashing the ether' means being played on the airwaves, I couldn't resist the irony."[151] The results of Keene's home studio recording were quite impressive. In contrast with recent releases, the album has a cleaner, jangly guitar sound that harkens back to Keene's '80s-era recordings for Dolphin and Geffen. "People were saying, 'These guitars sound so great. Why don't you use those cleaner sounds again?'" Keene said. "I've always had kind of a dual sound, both clean and dirty. But on this record, I just tried to mix up the guitar sounds more."[152] The album also features a sharp, powerful drum sound, which was achieved by recording the drums in the high-ceilinged foyer of Keene's house. "You walk in the place, and there's a tall, really high ceiling in the entryway," Keene noted. "As soon as I moved in the house, John said 'Man, you've got to record the drums here.' And it sounded great. There's no reverb dialed in, it's all natural ambience."[153]

The album kicks off with two great back-to-back pop anthems, "Black & White New York" and "Warren in the '60s," both of which feature jangly guitar and catchy, sing-along refrains. "Wishing" and "Eyes of Youth" are also jangly pop-rock numbers. "Driving Down the Road in My Mind" is an epic ballad that builds to a climax with a powerful guitar solo. On "Lives Become Lies," Keene lays a beautiful, ethereal melody over a slow-burning dance groove. "I've Heard That Wind Blow Before" is a psychedelic-tinged number, highlighted by the interplay between Keene's hard-edged guitar and John Richardson's thundering drums.

The album again received a positive reaction from the press. "With its anthemic sweep and a flurry of irresistible refrains, songs such as 'Black & White New York,' 'Wishing,' 'Lives Become Lies,' and 'Eyes of Youth' rank among the most riveting compositions Keene's ever offered," Lee Zimmerman wrote in *Amplifier*. "This, his tenth album, sounds as vital as his first with its vivid imagery, pulsating percussion, and a rich sonic sheen that finds each track practically leaping out at the listener."[154] Writing in *Playback St. Louis*, Laura Hamlet stated that "Everything you've come to expect from a Tommy Keene record is here: jangly, crashing guitars, power-pop precision, lyrical wordplay, that nasally yet completely one-of-a-kind voice."[155]

In May, Keene's collaboration with Robert Pollard was released under the title *Blues and Boogie Shoes*, with Keene and Pollard billed as the "Keene Brothers." "Bob came up with the name which I thought was funny because I have an older brother Bobby and of course we are known as Bobby and Tommy Keene," Keene stated.[156] The album was released as #42 in Pollard's "Fading Captain" series.

The collaboration proved to be a strong one, successfully combining Keene's pop smarts with Pollard's quirky wordplay. The album is highlighted by catchy, anthemic rockers like "Beauty of the Draft," "Heaven's Gate," and "This Time Do You Feel it?" and the ballad "Island of Lost Lucys," with Pollard singing over a bed of chiming acoustic and electric guitars.

During June, Keene toured in support of the *Crashing the Ether* album, with a band that consisted of John Richardson on drums, Paul Chastain (of Velvet Crush) on bass, and Dave Phillips (of the Pollard band) on guitar. In July, Keene played a few more dates as a member of the Robert Pollard band, including a couple of arena shows opening for Pearl Jam. In late September, Keene did a three-date Midwestern tour with his own band, with Brad Quinn returning on bass. As of this writing, Keene is scheduled to tour as part of the Robert Pollard band during the fall in support of Pollard's new album, *Normal Happiness*.

While Keene has expressed frustration with the music business in the past, the events of the past year seem to have lifted his morale. "I'm having a much better time," Keene said recently. "My morale is way up, thanks to the Pollard tour. Two years ago, I was thinking, 'Ugh, can I keep doing this? Is it time to call it?' But we're about to go on tour to San Francisco, Chicago, Minneapolis, New York, Philadelphia, Boston. I'm almost at a career high right now. If this is as good as it gets, I'm fine with it. Right now I'm happy—I'm satisfied for the first time in a while. And the Pollard band is the best band I've ever played with."[157]

"I'm 47 and I just feel lucky that I'm still doing it," Keene also said recently. "I've worked with the guys I consider the two best songwriters of my generation in Bob Pollard and Paul Westerberg. And people are still eager to put my records out. It's all a gift. It could be a lot worse."[158]

If the past in any indication, we will be hearing lots more great music from Tommy Keene in the years to come.

End Notes

1. Harrington, "The Big Breakout," p. K6 and "Out of the Ether"; and Opsas-nick, *Capitol Rock*, p. 117.

2. Harcourt.

3. Bass, "Relax, It's Only a Movie," p.13; Cost, p. 12; and Harcourt.

4. Harcourt.

5. Cost, p. 12.

6. Cabin, "Tommy Keene Throws an Isolation Party, Part Two," p. 16.

7. *Id.*

8. *Id.*

9. Cost, p. 12.

10. *Id.*

11. Cabin, "Tommy Keene Throws an Isolation Party, Part Two," p. 16–p. 17.

12. *Id.*

13. Cost, p. 12; and Hamlet, "Tommy Keene: Why His Music Matters".

14. Bubblegum the Pop.

15. Romanelli, p. 26.

16. Bubblegum the Pop.

17. Cost, p. 12; and Romanelli, p. 26.

18. Cost, p. 12.

19. Cabin, "Tommy Keene Throws an Isolation Party, Part Two," p. 17.

20. Mudd, p. 28; and Opsasnick, *Capitol Rock*, p. 117.

21. Opsasnick, *Capitol Rock*, p. 110–p. 115.

22. Opsasnick, *Capitol Rock*, p. 115.

23. Opsasnick, *Capitol Rock*, p. 115–p. 116.

24. Bounds, p. 23; and Opsasnick, *Capitol Rock*, p. 115–p. 116.

25. Opsasnick, *Capitol Rock*, p. 116.

26. Opsasnick, *Capitol Rock*, p. 117.

27. *Id.*

28. Bass, "Relax, It's Only a Movie," p. 13.

29. Opsasnick, *Capitol Rock*, p. 118.

30. *Id.*

31. Mudd, p. 28.

32. Opsasnick, *Capitol Rock*, p. 130.

33. Cost, p. 12.

34. Opsasnick, *Capitol Rock*, p. 121.

35. Harrington, "Rocking Around Washington," p. H3; and Opsasnick, *Capitol Rock*, p.113–p. 114.

36. Opsasnick, *Capitol Rock*, p. 121–p. 122.

37. Cost, p. 12.

38. Mudd, p. 28.

39. Cabin, "Tommy Keene Throws an Isolation Party, Part Two," p. 18.

40. Cabin, "Tommy Keene Throws an Isolation Party, Part Two," p. 17–p. 18.

41. Cabin, "Tommy Keene Throws an Isolation party, Part Two," p. 18.

42. Opsasnick, *Capitol Rock*, p. 255.

43. Harrington, "Rocking Around Washington," p. H3.

44. Gershon.

45. Musician and production credits for *Strange Alliance*.

46. Standish, p. 88.

47. Sasfy, "Up with Local Rock," p. B15.

48. Yockel, "(Almost) Perfect 10," p. 21.

49. Bloomquist, p. 13.

50. Bloomquist, p. 14.

51. Iannucci, p. 43–p. 44; Kelly and Phillips, p. 34–p. 35; and Warner, p. 15.

52. Harrington, "WHFS," p. G1.

53. Gershon.

54. Fufkin.

55. Hermon, "Gatecrashing the Isolation Party," p. 13.

56. Gershon.

57. Musician and production credits for *Places That Are Gone*.

58. Bounds, p. 23; and Pierson, p. 25.

59. Cabin, "In the Real Underground, Part Two," p. 2.

60. Sasfy, "Home Grown Tunes," p. B6.

61. Yockel, "Peachy Keene," p. 22–p. 23.

62. Harrington, "The Big Breakout," p. K1, p. K6, and K7.

63. "The 1984 Pazz & Jop Critics' Poll," *The Village Voice*, February 19, 1985; and Puterbaugh, "*Places That Are Gone*," p. 55.

64. Hermon, "Gatecrashing the Isolation Party," p. 13.

65. Borack, liner notes for CD reissue of *Songs from the Film*; Puterbaugh, "Tommy Keene's Picture Perfect Pop," p. 20; and musician and production credits for *Run Now*.

66. Keene, posting on message board at www.TommyKeene.com, 8/19/02.

67. Gershon.

68. Musician and production credits for "Back Again (Try …)."

69. Bass, "Relax It's Only a Movie," p. 12; Cost, p. 13; and Hermon, "Gatecrashing the Isolation Party," p. 13.

70. *Id.*

71. Hermon, "Gatecrashing the Isolation Party," p. 13.

72. Bass, "Relax It's Only a Movie," p. 13.

73. Musician and production credits for *Songs from the Film* .

74. Bass, "Relax, It's Only a Movie," p. 13; Larson, p. 16; Mudd, p. 28; and Orbezua.

75. Bass, "Relax, It's Only a Movie," p. 13.

76. Larson, p. 13.

77. Bass, "Relax, It's Only a Movie," p. 13; Hermon, "Gatecrashing the Isolation Party," p. 13; and musician and production credits for *Songs from the Film.*

78. Musician and production credits for *Songs from the Film.*

79. Sasfy, "Tommy Keene, D.C.'s Rocker," p. G5.

80. Himes, p. W23.

81. Yockel, "Lean Keene."

82. Considine, "Tommy Keene: With New Album he Faces the Music Scene," p. 14B.

83. Tannenbaum.

84. Bass, "Those Low Down Payola Blues," p. 13; Considine, "The Flip Side of Fame," p. B7; and Larson, p. 16.

85. Larson, p. 16.

86. Production credits for "Places That Are Gone" b/w "Faith in Love."

87. Bass, "Relax, It's Only a Movie," p. 13; and Larson, p. 16.

88. Tommy Keene Information Service Newsletter, p. 1–p. 2.

89. Whitburn, p. 380.

90. Musician and production credits for *Run Now.*

91. Mehr, p. 37.

92. Considine, "The Flip Side of Fame," p. B7; Cost, p. 13; and "Tommy Keene *Run Now* mini album."

93. "Tommy Keene *Run Now* mini album."

94. *Id.*

95. Considine, "The Flip Side of Fame," p. B7.

96. Larson, p. 16.

97. Opsasnick, *Capitol Rock*, p. 121.

98. "Tommy Keene: The History"; and Yockel, "Twist & Shout: Tommy Keene Comes Clean."

99. Musician and production credits for *Based on Happy Times.*

100. Keene, liner notes for *Drowning*; "Tommy Keene: The History"; and Yockel, "Twist & Shout: Tommy Keene Comes Clean."

101. "Tommy Keene: The Record."

102. Anft, "The Pop Report," p. E7.

103. McCormick.

104. Cost, p. 13; and Larson, p. 16.

105. Mehr, "The Lifer."

106. *Id.*

107.Whitburn, p. 380.

108.Fufkin; Orbezua; and Pierson, p. 26.

109.Orbezua.

110.Musician and production credits for *Illiterature*.

111.Considine, *"Sleeping on a Rollercoaster."*

112.Bloomquist, p. 12–p. 13.

113.Bloomquist, p. 17.

114.Keene, posting on message board at www.TommyKeene.com, 1/14/05.

115.Fufkin.

116.Musician and production credits for *Ten Years After*.

117.*Id.*

118.Orbezua.

119.Considine, *"Ten Years After,"* p. 7.

120.Hermon, *"Ten Years After,"* p. 5.

121.Musician and production credits for *Ten Years After*.

122.*Id.*

123.*Id.*

124.Cabin, "Tommy Keene Throws an Isolation Party, Part One," p. 17.

125.Kane.

126.Cabin, "Catching Up with Tommy Keene, p. 15.

127.*Id.*

128.*Id.*

129. Cabin, "Catching Up with Tommy Keene," p. 15–p. 17.

130. Cabin, "Catching Up with Tommy Keene," p. 17.

131. *Id.*

132. *Id.*

133. *Id.*

134. Musician and production credits for *The Merry-Go-Round Broke Down.*

135. *Id.*

136. Cabin, "Catching Up with Tommy Keene," p. 14.

137. *Id.*

138. *Id.*

139. *Id.*

140. Holmes, p. 27.

141. "New Tommy Keene Studio Album"; and musician and production credits for *Crashing the Ether.*

142. Musician and production credits for *Crashing the Ether.*

143. *Id.*

144. "New Tommy Keene Studio Album."

145. Weigal, "Back to Happy Times Again."

146. Hamlet, "Tommy Keene | Happy Times."

147. Musician and production credits for *Blues and Boogie Shoes.*

148. *Id.*

149. *Id.*

150. Weigal, "Back to Happy Times Again."

151.Trunk.

152.LeRoy.

153.Harrington, "Out of the Ether."

154.Zimmerman, *Crashing the Ether*," p. 47.

155.Hamlet, "*Crashing the Ether.*"

156.Trunk.

157.Weigal, "Back to Happy Times Again."

158.Mehr, "On the Record," p. 37.

II. Bibliography

Thanks to Mark Opsasnick and Wendy Shea for their contributions to this bibliography.

Books

Bianco, David; *Who's New Wave in Music: An Illustrated Encyclopedia, 1976–1982, The First Wave*; Popular Culture, Ink; Ann Arbor, MI; 1985.

Opsasnick, Mark; *Capitol Rock*; Fort Center Books; Riverdale, MD; 1996.

—; *Washington Rock and Roll: A Social History*; Fort Center Books; Riverdale, MD 1998.

Whitburn, Joel; *Joel Whitburn's Top Pop Albums 1955–1992*; Record Research, Inc.; Menomonee Falls, WI; 1993.

Articles/Interviews

Anonymous; "Tommy Keene Organizes His Own *Party*"; SonicNet Daily Music News Reports; April 3, 1998.

Baker, Brian; "Tommy Keene: Keene Instincts"; *Harp*; September/October 2002: www.harpmagazine.com.

Bass, Brad; "Relax, It's Only a Movie"; *The Choice*; April 1986: 12–13.

—; "Those Low Down Payola Blues"; *The Choice*; April 1986: 12.

Behe, Regis; "Tommy Keene Continues Signature Style"; *Pittsburgh Tribune-Review*; June 15, 2006: www.pittsburghlive.com.

Benjamin, Kelly; "Mr. Inconspicuous: Tommy Keene's Legend Remains in the Shadows"; *Scene*; May 14–20, 1998: 27.

Bloomquist, Randall; "Broadcast Blues: WHFS Adapts to Competing in a Material World"; *The City Paper* (Baltimore); April 12, 1991: 12–19.

Bounds, Mark; "Ted Niceley: Producing Results"; *The Music Monthly*; October 1990: 23.

Cabin, Geoff; "Catching Up with Tommy Keene"; *Rock Beat International*; Issue No. 23, Spring 2003: 13–18.

—; "Tommy Keene Throws an Isolation Party, Part Two"; *Rock Beat International*; Issue No. 15, Fall 1998: 16–19.

—; "Tommy Keene Throws an Isolation Party, Part One"; *Rock Beat International*; Issue No. 14, Summer 1998: 16–21.

—; "Tommy Keene: In the Real Underground, Part Four"; *Rock Beat International*; Issue No. 4, Spring 1995: 3–9.

—; "Tommy Keene: In the Real Underground, Part Three"; *On the Beat*; Issue No. 3, Winter 1994/95: 1–5.

—; "Tommy Keene: In the Real Underground, Part Two"; *On the Beat*; Issue No. 2, Fall 1994: 1–4.

—; "Tommy Keene: In the Real Underground, Part One"; *On the Beat*; Issue No. 1, Summer 1994: 1-4.

Considine, J.D.; "The Flip Side of Fame: Tommy Keene: Good Press, But Not Here"; *The Washington Post*; November 19, 1986: B7.

—; "Tommy Keene: With New Album He Faces the Music Scene"; *The Sun* (Baltimore); March 14, 1986: B1 and B14.

Cost, Jud; "Can You Hear Me? Jud Cost Interviews Tommy Keene"; *The Bob*; c. Fall 1996: 12–13.

Devenish, Colin; "Tommy Keene Gets Merry: With Help from Jay Bennett, Rocker Adds 'Oddball Sounds' to New Set"; wwwrollingstone.com: April 2, 2002.

Dominic; Serene; "That '80s Sound: With Help from Wilco and the Gin Blossoms, Tommy Keene Chases Down the Sound He Was After 20 Years Ago"; *Phoenix New Times*; August 15, 2002: www.phoenixnewtimes.com.

Fufkin, David; "The Tommy Keene Interview"; Fufkin.com: June 2002.

Gross, Jason; "Tommy Keene: Keene and Able"; *Harp*; July/August 2006: harpmagazine.com.

Hamlet, Laura; "Tommy Keene/Happy Times"; *Playback St. Louis*; May 22, 2006: www.playbackstl.com.

—; "Tommy Keene: Why His Music Matters!"; *Playback St. Louis*; c. Summer 2002: www.playbackstl.com/Current/Archive/tommykeene.htm.

Harcourt, Nick; on-air interview with Tommy Keene on "Morning Becomes Eclectic"; KCRW, Santa Monica, CA; May 28, 1998.

Harrington, Richard; "Keene: Out of the Ether But Still on the Edge"; *The Washington Post*; June 16, 2006: W10.

—; "The Big Breakout: Tommy Keene and His Escape from Washington"; *The Washington Post*; June 3, 1984: K1, K6, and K7.

—; "WHFS: The End of the Rainbow;" *The Washington Post*; January 16, 1983: G1 and G6.

Heller, Greg; "Alone Again, Naturally'; *BAM*; May 22, 1998: 25.

Hermon, Terry: "Gatecrashing the Isolation Party: Terry Hermon Meets Up with Guitar-Pop Icon Tommy Keene"; *Bucketfull of Brains*; Issue No. 51: 12–14.

Hickey, Matt; "Restoring the Classics: Tommy Keene's *Songs from the Film* Is Finally Released on CD"; *Magnet*; Issue no. 36, September/October 1998.

—; "Party of One: Tommy Keene"; *Magnet*; c. Winter/Spring 1998: 25.

Iannucci, Lisa; "Cerphe: WHFS, Washington DC"; *Backstreets*; Issue No. 82, Spring 2005: 43–44.

Jenkins, Mark; "The Re-Form Party: Dinosaurs of D.C. Rock Resurrected"; *City Paper* (Washington, D.C.); August 4, 2006: www.washingtoncitypaper.com

Keene, Tommy; "Mix It Up"; *Amplifier*, Issue #54; p. 21.

Kelly, John J. and Christopher Phillips; "Hey Mr. Deejay!"; *Backstreets*; Issue No. 82, Spring 2005: 34–35.

Koepenick, Sean; "Interview with Tommy Keene"; *Ear Candy*, October 2006; www.earcandymag.com/tommykeene-2006.htm.

—; "Tommy Keene"; *Ear Candy*, August 2002: www.earcandymag.com.

Lanham, Tom; "Tommy Keene: Back Again, Trying …"; *Pulse*; April 1996: 34.

Larson, John, "Tommy Keene: The Real Underground"; *Amplifier*, Volume 2, No. 1: 14–16.

LeRoy, Dan; "Tommy Keene Plans Two New Albums"; www.billboard.com: January 17, 2006.

Mehr, Bob; "The Lifer: Tommy Keene Should Be Famous, But He's Not Gonna Quit Just Because He Isn't"; *Chicago Reader*, June 16, 2006: www.chicagoreader.com.

—; "On the Record: A Conversation with … Tommy Keene"; *Magnet*, No. 71, April/May 2006: 36–37.

Mudd, Susan E.; "Tommy Keene: Earning His Piece of the Pie"; *Maryland Musician Magazine*; April 1989: 28–29.

Orbezua, Inaki; "Tommy Keene"; *Otono Cheyenne*; Issue No. 2.

Pierson, Pat; "Tommy Keene!!!"; *Yellow Pills*; Issue No. 2: 25–26.

Puterbaugh, Parke; "Tommy Keene's Picture-Perfect Pop: Washington Rocker Takes a Stab at the Big Time"; *Rolling Stone*; July 3, 1986: 20.

Reighley, Kurt B.; "Pop Purist: Tommy Keene Isn't Just Another Boy in the Bland"; *Paper*; c. Winter 1996: 120.

Romanelli, Steve; "Richard X. Heyman: From Rage to Riches"; *The Music Monthly*; November 1990: 26–27.

Standish, Peter; "Tommy Keene"; *Rolling Stone*; c. September 1985: 88.

van Alstyne, Rob; "Tommy Keene: Pop for the Ages"; *Pulse of the Twin Cities*; August 21, 2002: wwwpulsetc.com.

Warner, Tom; "Q&A: Jonathan S. Gilbert"; *The City Paper* (Baltimore); August 3, 1984: 14–15.

Watanabe, Mutsuo; "Tommy Keene"; *jem*; Issue No. 6, Fall 1996: 14–15.

Weigal, David; "Back to Happy Times Again: An Interview with Tommy Keene"; www.popmatters.com: March 28, 2006.

Wilder, Eliot; "Tommy Keene: Life Is a Carousel"; *Amplifier*; Issue No. 31: 42–43.

Wright, Rickey; "Back Again"; *The City Paper* (Washington, D.C.); February 27, 1998: 38.

Yockel, Michael; "Twist & Shout: Tommy Keene Comes Clean"; *The City Paper* (Baltimore); c. March 1989.

Liner Notes

Borack, John M.; liner notes for CD reissue of *Songs from the Film* by Tommy Keene; Geffen Records; 1998.

Einstein, David; liner notes for *Strange Alliance* by Tommy Keene; Avenue Records; 1982.

Gershon, Rick; liner notes for *The Real Underground* by Tommy Keene; Alias Records; 1993.

Keene, Tommy; liner notes for *Drowning: A Tommy Keene Miscellany* by Tommy Keene; Not Lame Records; 2004.

Press Releases/Promotional Material

"Tommy Keene"; Geffen Records biography; 1986.

"Tommy Keene *Run Now* mini-album"; Geffen Records promotional material; 1986.

"Tommy Keene Information Service Newsletter"; February 1987.

"Tommy Keene: The History"; Geffen Records biography; 1989.

"Tommy Keene: The Record" Geffen Records promotional material; 1989.

"Tommy Keene: Ten Years After"; Matador Records biography; 1996.

"Tommy Keene: Isolation Party"; Matador Records promotional material; 1998.

"Tommy Keene Factsheet!"; Matador Records promotional material; 1998.

"Tommy Keene: *Showtunes: The Live Tommy Keene Album*; Parasol Publicity promotional material; 2001.

"New Tommy Keene Studio Album Due Apr. 4 on Eleven Thirty Records"; Eleven Thirty Records promotional material; 2006.

"Tommy Keene"; Eleven Thirty Records biography; 2006.

Record Reviews

Connected

Harrington, Richard; "Rocking Around Washington"; *The Washington Post*; November 22, 1981: H3.

Strange Alliance

Considine, J.D.; "Tommy Keene: *Strange Alliance*"; *Musician*; c. Summer 1982: 108.

Sasfy, Joe; "Up with Local Rock"; *The Washington Post*; July 28, 1982: B15.

Yockel, Michael; "(Almost) Perfect 10"; *The City Paper* (Baltimore); June 25, 1982: 21.

Places That Are Gone

Christgau, Robert; "Tommy Keene: *Places That Are Gone*"; *Christgau's Consumer Guide*; c. Spring 1984: www.robertchristgau.com.

Puterbaugh, Parke; "*Places That Are Gone*/'Back Again (Try ...)' by Tommy Keene"; *Rolling Stone*; February 28, 1985: 55.

Sasfy, Joe; "Home-Grown Tunes"; *The Washington Post*; April 26, 1984: B6.

Yockel, Michael; "Peachy Keene; Ravyns Cave In"; *The City Paper*; April 13, 1984: 22–23.

"Back Again (Try ...)"

Puterbaugh, Parke; "*Places That Are Gone*/'Back Again (Try ...)' by Tommy Keene"; *Rolling Stone*; February 28, 1985: 55.

Sasfy, Joe; "Tommy Keene: Stardom on Hold"; *The Washington Post*; January 18, 1985: W39.

Songs from the Film

Considine, J.D.; "Tommy Keene: *Songs from the Film*"; *Musician*; c. Winter 1986: 92.

Sasfy, Joe; "Tommy Keene, D.C.'s Rocker"; *The Washington Post*; March 2, 1986: G1 and G5.

Tannenbaum, Rob; "Tommy Keene: *Songs from the Film*"; *Rolling Stone*; Issue No. 424.

Yockel, Michael; "Lean Keene"; *The City Paper* (Baltimore); c. March 1986.

Run Now

Himes, Geoffrey; "Local Bands: Pressing On"; *The Washington Post*; November 28, 1986: W23.

Based on Happy Times

Anft, Michael; "The Pop Report: Local Troopers Hoping to Break Baltimore Recording Jinx"; *The Evening Sun* (Baltimore); February 23, 1989: E7.

McCormick, Moira; "Tommy Keene: *Based on Happy Times*"; *Rolling Stone*; Issue No. 554.

Sleeping on a Rollercoaster

Baker, Brain; "*Sleeping on a Rollercoaster*: Tommy Keene"; *Everybody's News*; October 8–21, 1993.

Borack, John M.; "Tommy Keene: *Sleeping on a Rollercoaster*"; *Goldmine*; March 18, 1994: 62 and 64.

Considine, J.D.; "Tommy Keene: *Sleeping on a Rollercoaster*"; *Musician*; February 1983.

Erwin, G.W.; "Tommy Keene: *Sleeping on a Rollercoaster*"; *Alternative Press*; February 1993.

Wiederhorn, Jon; "Tommy Keene: *Sleeping on a Rolleercoaster*"; *CMJ*; October 30, 1992.

The Real Underground

Anderson, Lydia; "Tommy Keene: *The Real Underground*"; *CMJ*; September 20, 1993.

Baker, Brian; "*The Real Underground*: Tommy Keene"; *Everybody's News*; October 8–21, 1993.

Borack, John M.; "Tommy Keene: *The Real Underground*"; *Goldmine*; July 8, 1994: 164.

Braitman, Stephen M.H.; "Tommy Keene: *The Real Underground*"; *Alternative Press*; January 1994.

Hickey, Matt; "Tommy Keene: *The Real Underground*"; *Magnet*; c. Summer/Fall 1993.

Huffman, Eddie; "Tommy Keene: *The Real Underground*"; *Option*; January/February 1994: 112.

Woodlief, Mark; "Tommy Keene: *The Real Underground*"; *The Bob*; c. Summer/Fall 1993.

Driving into the Sun

Cranna, Ian; "Tommy Keene: *Driving into the Sun*"; *Q*; c. Winter/Spring 1995: 135.

sing HOLLIES in reverse

Cabin, Geoff, "*sing HOLLIES in reverse*: various artists"; *Rock Beat International*; Issue No. 6, Fall 1995: 17–18.

Henderson, Anthony; "Various: *Sing HOLLIES in Reverse*"; *Audities*; November—December 1995: 11.

Ten Years After

Anft, Michael; "Tommy Keene: *Ten Years After*; *The City Paper* (Baltimore); May 29, 1996: 28.

Auker, John; "Tommy Keene: *Ten Years After*"; *Pallid Pilgrim*; Volume 2, No.6, Winter 1996/1997: 10–11.

Borack, John M.; "Tommy Keene: *Ten Years After*"; *Goldmine*; Issue No. 46, July 5, 1996: 90.

Cabin, Geoff; "*Ten Years After*: Tommy Keene"; *Rock Beat International*; Issue No. 8, Summer 1996: 17–18.

Considine, J.D.; "*Ten Years After*: Tommy Keene"; *The Sun* (Baltimore); February 22, 1996: L7.

Hermon, Terry; "Tommy Keene: *Ten Years After*"; *Audities*; May—June 1996: 5 and 9.

Pierson, Pat; "Tommy Keene: *Ten Years After*"; *Yeah, Yeah, Yeah*; May—June 1996: 38–39.

Sheridan, Phil; "Tommy Keene: *Ten Years After*"; *Magnet*; c. Winter/Spring 1998.

Isolation Party

Arnold, Gina; "Tommy Keene: *Isolation Party*"; *Salon*; February 26, 1998: www.salon.com.

Auker, John; "Tommy Keene: *Isolation Party*"; *Pallid Pilgrim*; Volume 2, No. 8, Winter 1998–1999: 19.

Borack, John M.; "Tommy Keene: *Isolation Party*"; *Goldmine*; Issue no. 462, April 10, 1998: 130.

Cabin, Geoff; "*Isolation Party*: Tommy Keene"; *Rock Beat International*; Issue No. 14, Summer 1998: 29–30.

Hermon, Terry; "Tommy Keene: *Isolation Party*"; *Bucketfull of Brains*; Issue No. 50: 25.

Kane, Peter; "Tommy Keene: *Isolation Party*"; *Q*; c. Winter/Spring 1998: 102.

Naporano, F.; "Tommy Keene: *Isolation Party*"; *POPsided*; c. Winter/Spring 1998: 10.

Wilonsky, Robert; "… Different Year"; *New Times Los Angeles*; February 19–25, 1998: 58.

Songs from the Film (1998 CD reissue)

Cabin, Geoff; "*Songs from the Film*: Tommy Keene"; *Rock Beat International*; Issue No. 15, Fall 1998: 36–37.

Hermon, Terry; "Tommy Keene: *Songs from the Film*"; *Bucketfull of Brains*; Issue No. 52: 27.

Showtunes

Bennett, Mike; "Tommy Keene—*Showtunes*; Fufkin.com; October 2001: www.fufkin.com.

Cabin, Geoff; "*Showtunes*: Tommy Keene"; *Rock Beat International*; Issue No. 22, Fall 2002: 26.

Griffith, Jackson; "Tommy Keene: *Showtunes*"; *Sacramento News and Review*; January 3, 2002: www.newsreview.com/sacramento

Naporano, Fernando; "Tommy Keene: *Showtunes*"; *Bucketfull of Brains*; Issue No. 60: 28.

Wilder, Eliot; "Tommy Keene: *Showtunes*; *Amplifier*; Issue No. 26: 60.

The Merry-Go-Round Broke Down

Cabin, Geoff; "*The Merry-Go-Round Broke Down*: Tommy Keene"; *Rock Beat International*; Issue No. 23, Spring 2003: 20–21.

Cloutier, Cecile; "Tommy Keene: *The Merry-Go-Round Broke Down*"; *City Pages*; August 28, 2002: www.citypages.com

Holmes, Bill; "Tommy Keene: *The Merry-Go-Round Broke Down*"; *Bucketfull of Brains*; Issue No. 62: 27.

Jenkins, Mark; "Tommy Keene: *The Merry-Go-Round Broke Down*; *The Washington Post*; August 23, 2002: W8.

Sullivan, Denise; "Tommy Keene: *The Merry-Go-Round Broke Down*"; www.rollingstone.com; June 4, 2002.

Drowning: A Tommy Keene Miscellany

Cabin, Geoff; "*Drowning*: Tommy Keene"; *Rock Beat International*; Issue No. 26, Spring 2005: 18.

Hermon, Terry; "Tommy Keene: *Drowning—A Tommy Keene Miscellany*'; *Bucketfull of Brains*; Issue No 67: 27.

Hinely, Tim; "Tommy Keene—*Drowning: A Tommy Keene Miscellany*"; *Dagger*; Issue No. 36, Spring 2005.

Stacey, John; "Tommy Keene | *Miscellany*"; *Comes with a Smile*; November—December 2004; cwas.hinah.com

Zimmerman, Lee; "Tommy Keene: *Drowning/A Tommy Keene Miscellany*"; *Amplifier*, Issue No. 45: 67–69.

Crashing the Ether

Benjamin, Kent H.; "Tommy Keene: *Crashing the Ether*; *Pop Culture Press*; Issue 62, Spring & Summer 2006: 46

Forsman, Matt; "Tommy Keene—*Crashing the Ether*"; *SF Station*; April 7, 2006: www.sfstation.com.

Francis, Susan; "Tommy Keene: *Crashing the Ether*"; *Hybrid Magazine*; www.hybridmagazine.com.

Gladstone, E.C.; "Tommy Keene—*Crashing the Ether*"; *Rhino Magazine*; #801: www.rhino.com.

Hamlet, Laura; "Tommy Keene: *Crashing the Ether*"; *Playback St Louis*; April 25, 2006: www.playbackstl.com.

Holmes, Bill; "Tommy Keene: *Crashing the Ether*"; *Bucketfull of Brains*; Issue #69, Spring 2006: 29.

MacIntosh, Dan; "Tommy Keene: *Crashing the Ether*"; *Pop Matters*; July 31, 2006: www.popmatters.com.

O'Connor, Rob; "Tommy Keene: *Crashing the Ether*; americanwired.com/music/ April06 music/musicreviewsdetail.html.

Simpson, Doug; "Tommy Keene: *Crashing the Ether*"; www.campuscircle.net/ reviews. cfm?r=2195.

Strub, Whitney; "Tommy Keene: *Crashing the Ether*"; *Stylus*; April 10, 2006: www.stylusmagazine.com.

Valich, Frank; "Tommy Keene: *Crashing the Ether*"; *Under the Radar*; www.undertheradarmag.com.

Zimmerman, Lee; "Tommy Keene: *Crashing the Ether*"; *Amplifier*, Issue #54: 47.

Blues and Boogie Shoes

Bennett, Mike; "Keene Brothers: *Blues and Boogie Shoes*"; Fufkin.com; August/ September 2006: www.fufkin.com.

Heaton, Dave; "Keene Brothers—*Blues and Boogie Shoes*"; *The Big Takeover*; June 3, 2006: www.bigtakeover.com.

Websites

Official Tommy Keene Website:
   www.TommyKeene.com

Tommy Keene MySpace site:
   www.myspace.com/tommykeene

Allmusic:
   www.allmusic.com/cg/amg.d11?p=amg&sql=11:7wsqoauabijn

Bubblegum the Punk: Guide to Powerpop Bands (North America 1975–'82):
   www.geocities.com/SunsetStrip/Venue/6041/pp-dg11.html

Bug Music:
   www.bugmusic.com

Eleven Thirty Records:
   www.eleventhirtyrecords.com/artist_info.php?artistid=611

Matador Records:
   www.matadorrecords.com/tommy_keene/index.html

Not Lame Recordings:
   www.notlame.com/Tommy_Keene/Page_1/NLKEE1.html

Parasol Records:
   www.parasol.com

Rolling Stone magazine:
   www.rollingstone.com/tommykeene

spinART Records:
 www.spinart records.com/site/bandpage.php?id=30

30 Under DC: Punk Rock in Washington, 1975–2005:
 www.30underdc.com

Trouser Press:
 www.trouserpress.com/entry.php?a=tommy_keene&tr=y

Wikipedia:
 en.wikipedia.org/wiki/Tommy_Keene

III. Discography

Thanks to Steven Greenwood, Terry Hermon, and Troy Paterson for their contributions to this discography.

Solo
Albums and EPs

1982

Strange Alliance (Avenue)

Tommy Keene: vocals, guitars, keyboards, and all instruments on "Northern Lights."
Ted Nicely: bass guitar and percussion.
Doug Tull: drums.
Michael Colburn: harmony vocals on "Don't Get Me Wrong," "I Can't See You Anymore," and "Another Night at Home."

Produced by Ted Niceley and Tommy Keene.
Recorded by Jim Crenca and Mark Greenhouse at Track Recorders, Silver Spring, MD.

Side One:
1. "Landscape"
2. "All the Way Around"
3. "Don't Get Me Wrong"
4. "I Can't See You Anymore"

Side Two:
5. "It's All Happening Today"
6. "Strange Alliance"

7. "Another Night at Home"
8. Northern Lights"

All songs written by Tommy Keene.

1984

Places That Are Gone (Dolphin)

Tommy Keene: lead vocals and guitars.
Billy Connelly: vocals and guitars.
Ted Niceley: bass.
Doug Tull: drums.

Produced by Tommy Keene and Ted Niceley.
Recorded by Steve Carr at Hit and Run Studios, Rockville, MD.

Side One:
1. "Places That Are Gone"
2. "Nothing Happened Yesterday"
3. "Baby Face"

Side Two:
4. "Back to Zero Now"
5. "When the Truth Is Found"
6. "Hey! Little Child"

All songs written by Tommy Keene, except "Hey! Little Child," written by Alex Chilton.

1986

Songs from the Film (Geffen)

Tommy Keene: vocals, guitars, keyboards, and percussion.
Billy Connelly: guitars and background vocals.
Ted Niceley: bass.
Doug Tull: drums.

Produced by Geoff Emerick.

Engineered by Matt Butler.
Recorded at Air Studios, Montserrat, West Indies.

Side One:
1. "Places That Are Gone"
2. "In Our Lives"
3. "Listen to Me"
4. "Paper Words and Lies"
5. "Gold Town"
6. "Kill Your Sons"

Side Two:
7. "Call on Me"
8. "As Life Goes By"
9. "My Mother Looked Like Marilyn Monroe"
10. "Underworld"
11. "Astronomy"
12. "The Story Ends"

All songs written by Tommy Keene, except "Kill Your Sons," written by Lou Reed.

Note: *Songs from the Film* was reissued by Geffen on CD in 1998 with the following additional songs: "Run Now," "Away from It All," "I Don't Feel Right at All," "Back Again," and "They're in Their Own World" from the *Run Now* EP; "We're Two" and "Faith in Love" from the T-Bone Burnett/Don Dixon sessions for *Songs from the Film*; and "Take Back Your Letters" and "Teenage Head" from the Geoff Emerick sessions for *Songs from the Film*.

All additional songs written by Tommy Keene, except "Teenage Head," written by Roy Loney and Cyril Jordan.

Run Now (Geffen)

Tommy Keene: vocals, guitars, and keyboards.
Billy Connelly: guitar and background vocals.
Ted Niceley: bass and background vocals.
Doug Tull: drums.

Produced by T-Bone Burnett and Don Dixon and recorded at Reflection Studios, Charlotte, NC, August 1984.

"Run Now" produced by Bob Clearmountain and recorded at Bearsville Studios, Bearsville, NY, January 1986.

"Kill Your Sons" recorded live at the World, NYC, March 1986 and mixed by Jim Faraci.

Side One:
1. "Run Now"
2. "Away from It All"
3. "I Don't Feel Right at All"

Side Two:
4. "Back Again"
5. "They're in Their Own World"
6. "Kill Your Sons"

All songs written by Tommy Keene, except "Kill Your Sons," written by Lou Reed.

Note: All of the songs from the *Run Now* EP, except "Kill Your Sons," were included on the 1998 CD reissue of *Songs from the Film*.

1989

Based on Happy Times (Geffen)

Tommy Keene: vocals, guitars, and keyboards.
Joe Hardy: bass and keyboards.
John Hampton: drums and percussion.
Jules Shear: harmony vocal on "Nothing Can Change You" and "When Our Vows Break."
Jack Holder: guitar on "Light of Love," "When Our Vows Break," "The Biggest Conflict," and "If We Run Away."
Peter Buck: guitar on "Our Car Club" and mandolin on "A Way Out."
Greg "Fingers" Taylor: harmonica on "Our Car Club."
Jeff Jurciukonis: cello on "A Way Out."

Produced by Joe Hardy, John Hampton, and Tommy Keene.
Engineered by Joe Hardy and John Hampton.
Recorded and mixed at Ardent Studios, Memphis, TN.

Side One:
1. "Nothing Can Change You"
2. "Light of Love"
3. "This Could Be Fiction"
4. "Based on Happy Times"
5. "When Our Vows Break"
6. "The Biggest Conflict"

Side Two:
7. "Highwire Days"
8. "Our Car Club"
9. "If We Run Away"
10. "Hanging on to Yesterday"
11. "Pictures"
12. "A Way Out"

The CD version of the album contains an additional song, "Where Have All Your Friends Gone," that is not included on the vinyl or cassette versions of the album.

All songs written by Tommy Keene, except "When Our Vows Break" and "If We Run Away," written by Tommy Keene and Jules Shear, and "Our Car Club," written by Brian Wilson and Mike Love.

1991

Places That Are Gone (Demon) [U.K.] [cassette-only release]

Tommy Keene: lead vocals and guitars.
Billy Connelly: vocals and guitars.
Ted Niceley: bass.
Doug Tull: drums.

Produced by Tommy Keene and Ted Niceley.
Recorded by Steve Carr at Hit and Run Studios, Rockville, MD.

1. "Places That Are Gone"
2. "Nothing Happened Yesterday"
3. "Baby Face"
4. "Back to Zero Now"
5. When the Truth Is Found"
6. "Hey! Little Child"
7. "Something Got a Hold on Me"
8. "The Real Underground"
9. "The Scam and the Flim-Flam Man"
10. "Misunderstood"
11. "That You Do"
12. "Mr. Roland"

All songs written by Tommy Keene, except "Hey! Little Child," written by Alex Chilton.

Note: This is an expanded version of the *Places That Are Gone* EP. The first six songs comprise the original *Places That Are Gone* EP. "Something Got a Hold on Me," "The Real Underground," "Misunderstood," and "That You Do" are outtakes from the *Places That Are Gone* EP. "Mr. Roland" was originally released as the flipside of the "Back to Zero Now" single. "The Scam and the Flim-Flam Man" dates from around the time of *Songs from the Film*.

1992

Sleeping on a Rollercoaster (Matador)

Tommy Keene: vocals, guitars, and keyboards.
Brad Quinn: bass, vocals, and piano.
John Richardson: drums.
Justin Hibbard: guitar on "Driving into the Sun" and "Waiting to Fly."

Produced by Tommy Keene and Steve Carr.
Recorded by Steve Carr at Hit and Run Studios, Rockville, MD.
Mixed by John Hampton at Ardent Studios, Memphis, TN, except "Waiting to Fly," mixed at Hit and Run.

1. "Love Is a Dangerous Thing"

2. "Driving into the Sun"
3. "Down, Down, Down"
4. "Alive"
5. "Waiting to Fly"

All songs written by Tommy Keene.

1993

The Real Underground (Alias)

Tommy Keene: vocals, lead guitars, and keyboards.
Ted Niceley: bass on tracks 1–16.
Billy Connelly: guitar and vocals on tracks 1–13.
Doug Tull: drums on tracks 1–15.
Brad Quinn: bass and vocals on tracks 19–23.
John Richardson: drums on tracks 19–23.
Justin Hibbard: lead guitar on track 19 and rhythm guitar on tracks 21 and 23.
Eric Peterson: lead guitar on track 20 and second lead break on track 22.

Tracks 1–11 produced by Tommy Keene and Ted Niceley.
Recorded by Steve Carr at Hit and Run Studios, Rockville, MD.

Track 12 produced by T-Bone Burnett and Don Dixon.
Recorded at Reflection Studios, Charlotte, NC with Steve Haigler.

Track 13 produced by Don Dixon.
Remixed at TGS Studios, NC with Steve Gronback.

Tracks 14–23 produced by Tommy Keene.
Recorded by Steve Carr at Hit and Run Studios, Rockville, MD.

1. "Places That Are Gone"
2. "Nothing Happened Yesterday"
3. "Babyface"
4. "Back to Zero Now"
5. "When the Truth Is Found"
6. "Hey! Little Child"

7. "Something Got a Hold on Me"
8. "The Real Underground"
9. "Misunderstood"
10. "That You Do"
11. "Mr. Roland"
12. "Back Again"
13. "Safe in the Light"
14. "People with Fast Cars Drive Fast"
15. "Love Is the Only Thing That Matters"
16. "Dull Afternoon"
17. "Tattoo"
18. "Don't Sleep in the Daytime"
19. "Hey Man"
20. "Andrea"
21. "Something to Rave About"
22. "Shake Some Action"
23. "Sleeping on a Rollercoaster"

All songs written by Tommy Keene, except "Hey! Little Child," written by Alex Chilton, "Tattoo," written by Pete Townshend, and "Shake Some Action," written by Cyril Jordan and Chris Wilson.

Note: This is a compilation album that contains both previously-released material and previously-unereleased material. The first six songs comprise the original *Places That Are Gone* EP. "Mr. Roland" was released on the flipside of the "Back to Zero Now" single and "Back Again" and "Safe in the Light" were released on the "Back Again (Try …)" 12" single. "Something Got a Hold of Me," "The Real Underground," "Misunderstood," "That You Do," "People with Fast Cars Drive Fast," "Love Is the Only Thing That Matters," "Dull Afternoon," "Tattoo," and "Don't Sleep in the Daytime" are demos/outtakes that date from the mid-eighties. A few of these were previously released on the cassette-only expanded version of *Places That Are Gone* that was released by Demon in the U.K. "Hey Man," "Andrea," "Something to Rave About," "Shake Some Action," and "Sleeping on a Rollercoaster" are demos recorded from 1989 to 1991.

1994

Driving into the Sun (Alias) [U.K.]

Tommy Keene: vocals, lead guitars, and keyboards.
Brad Quinn: bass and vocals.
John Richardson: drums.
Eric Peterson: lead guitar on "Andrea."
Justin Hibbard: lead guitar on "Hey Man" and rhythm guitar on "Driving into the Sun," "Sleeping on a Rollercoaster," "Something to Rave About," "Tell Me Something," and "Waiting to Fly."
Ted Niceley: bass on "Love Is the Only Thing That Matters" and "Dull Afternoon."
Doug Tull: drums on "Love Is the Only Thing That Matters."

Recorded and mixed by Steve Carr at Hit and Run Studios, Rockville, MD.
"Love Is a Dangerous Thing," "Driving into the Sun," "Down, Down, Down," and "Alive" mixed by John Hampton at Ardent Studios, Memphis, TN.

1. "Hey Man"
2. "Love Is a Dangerous Thing"
3. "Driving into the Sun"
4. "Down, Down, Down"
5. "Sleeping on a Rollercoaster"
6. "Love Is the Only Thing That Matters"
7. "Dull Afternoon"
8. "Alive"
9. "Something to Rave About"
10. "Tattoo"
11. "Don't Sleep in the Daytime"
12. "Tell Me Something"
13. "Andrea"
14. "Waiting to Fly"

All songs written by Tommy Keene, except "Tattoo," written by Pete Townshend.

Note: This album contains all five songs from the *Sleeping on a Rollercoaster* EP, several songs from *The Real Underground*, and one song, "Tell Me Something," that was previously unreleased.

1996

Ten Years After (Matador)

Tommy Keene: vocals, guitars, and keyboards.
Brad Quinn: bass and vocals.
John Richardson: drums and percussion.
Adam Schmitt: backup vocals on "Going Out Again" and "Compromise" and bass on "Silent Town."
Jay Bennett: guitar on "Turning on Blue" and "We Started Over Again."
Justin Hibbard: guitar on "You Can't Wait for Time" and "Before the Lights Go Down."
Eric Peterson: guitar on "Your Heart Beats Alone."
Eric Heywood: pedal steel guitar on "If You're Getting Married Tonight."

Recorded and mixed by Adam Schmitt at Private Studios, Urbana, IL and Pachyderm, Cannon Falls, MN and by Steve Carr at Hit and Run Studios, Rockville, MD.

1. "Going Out Again"
2. "Turning on Blue"
3. "Today and Tomorrow"
4. "Your Heart Beats Alone"
5. "If You're Getting Married Tonight"
6. "On the Runway"
7. "We Started Over Again"
8. "Silent Town"
9. "Good Thing Going"
10. "Compromise"
11. "You Can't Wait for Time"
12. "Before the Lights Go Down"
13. "It's Not True" (unlisted bonus track)

The Japanese version of *Ten Years After* on the Bandai Music label contains two additional tracks, "Karl Marx" and "Soul Searching."

All songs written by Tommy Keene, except "It's Not True," written by Pete Townshend.

1998

Isolation Party (Matador)

Tommy Keene: vocals and guitars.

John Richardson: drums and percussion.

Jay Bennett: bass on tracks 4,5,6,7,8,9,11, and 12, organ on tracks 1, 4, 10, 12, and 13, acoustic guitar on tracks 8 and 12, and electric guitar on tracks 9 and 10.

Jeff Tweedy: backup vocals on "Never Really Been Gone" and "The World Outside."

Jesse Valenzuela: backup vocals on "Long Time Missing," "Getting Out from Under You," "Love Dies Down," and "Waiting Without You."

Leroy Bocchieri: bass on "Getting Out from Under You," "Take Me Back," "Tuesday Morning," and "Twilight's in Town."

Tom Broeske: bass on "Long Time Missing."

Josh Brookman: cello on "Twilight's in Town."

Recorded by Jeff Murphy at Short Order Recorders, Zion, IL and by Brendan Gamble, Jay Bennett, and Jonathan Pines at Private Studios, Urbana, IL.

Mixed by Jonathan Pines and Jay Bennett at Private Studios.

Production assistance by Jay Bennett and Jonathan Pines.

1. "Long Time Missing"
2. "Getting Out from Under You"
3. "Take Me Back"
4. "Never Really Been Gone"
5. "The World Outside"
6. "Einstein's Day"
7. "Battle Lines"
8. "Happy When You're Sad"
9. "Love Dies Down"
10. "Tuesday Morning"
11. "Waiting Without You"
12. "Weak and Watered Down"
13. "Twilight's in Town"

All songs written by Tommy Keene, except "Einstein's Day," written by Roger Miller.

2001

Showtunes

Tommy Keene: vocals and guitar.
Brad Quinn: bass and vocals.
John Richardson: drums.
Steve Gerlach: guitar, lead guitar on "Highwire Days."
Scott Johnson: guitar on "Silent Town," "Underworld," "My Mother Looked Like Marilyn Monroe," and "Back to Zero Now."

Recorded by Mike Leach in spring/summer 1998 and summer 2000.
Mixed by Jonathan Pines at Private Studios, Urbana, IL.

1. "Astronomy"/"This Could Be Fiction"
2. "Long Time Missing"
3. "Nothing Can Change You"
4. "Silent Town"
5. "Underworld"
6. "Going Out Again"
7. "Paper Words and Lies"
8. "My Mother Looked Like Marilyn Monroe"
9. "Einstein's Day"
10. "Highwire Days"
11. "When Our Vows Break"
12. "Compromise"
13. "Based on Happy Times"
14. "Back to Zero Now"
15. "Places That Are Gone"

All songs written by Tommy Keene, except "Einstein's Day," written by Roger Miller, and "When Our Vows Break," written by Tommy Keene and Jules Shear.

2002

The Merry-Go-Round Broke Down (spinART)

Tommy Keene: vocals and guitar.
Brad Quinn: bass and vocals.
John Richardson: drums and percussion.
Jay Bennett: keyboards.
Steve Gerlach: guitar on "Begin Where We End" and "The Final Hour."
Adam Schmitt: bass on "The World Where I Still Live."
Robin Wilson: vocal on "Time Will Take You Today."
Jesse Valenzuela: vocal on "Hanging Over Your Head."
Peter Roubal: tenor and baritone sax on "The Man Without a Soul" and "The World Where I Still Live" and horn arrangement on "The Man Without a Soul."
Jeff Hegelson: trumpet and flugelhorn on "The Man Without a Soul."
Kaz Machalla: French horn on "The Final Hour."

Recorded at Mayberry Studio in Tempe, AZ by Chris Widmer, Calle de Maria Studio in Palm Springs, CA by Tommy Keene, Private Studios in Urbana, IL by Jon Pines, Brendon Gamble, and Adam Schmitt, and Pieholden Studio in Chicago, IL by Jay Bennett.

Mixed at Private Studios by Jon Pines and Tommy Keene, except "The Final Hour," by Jon Pines, Jay Bennett, and Tommy Keene.

1. "Begin Where We End"
2. "The Man Without a Soul"
3. "Hanging Over My Head"
4. "All Your Love Will Stay"
5. "Technicolor"
6. "Big Blue Sky"
7. "The Final Hour"
8. "Time Will Take You Today"
9. "The World Where I Still Live"
10. "How Do You Really Say Hello?"
11. "Circumstance"
12. "The Fog Has Lifted"

All songs written by Tommy Keene.

2004

Drowning: A Tommy Keene Miscellany (Not Lame)

Tommy Keene: vocals, guitars, bass, keyboards, and lame drum machines.
Brad Quinn: bass and vocals on tracks 2, 3, 4, 15, and 16.
John Richardson: drums and percussion on tracks 1, 2, 3, 4, 15, and 16.
Ted Niceley: bass on tracks 5, 6, 10, 11, 12, 14, and 20.
Doug Tull: drums on tracks 10, 11, 12, 14, and 20.
Justin Hibbard: guitar on tracks 2, 3, 15, and 16, lead guitar on track 2.
Billy Connelly: guitar and vocals on tracks 14 and 20.
Jay Bennett: guitar on track 4.
Mike Leach: drums on tracks 7 and 8.
Jesse Valenzuela: guitar and vocals on track 13.
Phil Rhodes: drums and vocals on track 13.
Darryl Icard: drums on track 13.

Recorded by Steve Carr at Hit and Run Studios, Rockville, MD, except "Drowning" recorded by Chris Widmer at Mayberry Studio, Tempe, AZ and finished by Tommy Keene at home; "Carrie Anne" recorded by Billy Moss at Vintage Recorders, Phoenix, AZ and mixed by John Hampton at Ardent Studios, Memphis, TN; "Watch the World Go By" recorded at home by Tommy Keene; and "Drowning," "I'll Wait for You," and "Time to Say Goodbye" mixed by Jonathan Pines and Tommy Keene at Private Studios, Urbana, IL. Additional engineering on "Drowning," "I'll Wait for You," and "Time to Say Goodbye" by Mike Leach.

1. "Drowning"
2. "There's No One in This City"
3. "Tell Me Something"
4. "Karl Marx"
5. "When You Make Up Your Mind"
6. "You Won't Find Me"
7. "I'll Wait for You"
8. "Time to Say Goodbye"
9. "Where Have All Your Friends Gone"
10. "A Wish Ago"
11. "Everything Is One Thing"
12. "Lover's Lies"
13. "Carrie Anne"
14. "What Does It Matter to You"

15. "Disarray"
16. "Soul Searching"
17. "Watch the World Go By"
18. "We'll Always Remain Just the Same"
19. "I Know It's Blue"
20. "The Scam and the Flim-Flam Man"

All songs written by Tommy Keene, except "Carrie Anne," written by Alan Clarke, Tony Hicks, and Graham Nash.

<u>Note</u>: This is a rarities collection that contains both previously-released material and previously-unreleased material. "There's No One in This City" appeared on *The Bucketfull of Brains 50th Anniversary CD*; "Tell Me Something" appeared on the U.K.-only *Driving into the Sun*; "Karl Marx" and "Soul Searching" appeared on the Japanese version of *Ten Years After*; "Where Have All Your Friends Gone?" is a demo of the song that appeared as a bonus track on the CD version of *Based on Happy Times*; "Carrie Anne" appeared on *sing HOLLIES in reverse*; "Disarray" appeared on *Yellow Pills: The Best of American Pop, volume 1*; and "The Scam and the Flim-Flam man" appeared on the U.K. cassette-only release of *Places That Are Gone*.

2006

Crashing the Ether (Eleven Thirty)

Tommy Keene: vocals, guitars, bass, harmonica, and keyboards.
John Richardson: drums.
Brad Quinn: bass on "I've Heard That Wind Blow Before."
Steve Gerlach: guitar solo on "Wishing."
Jesse Valenzuela: harmony vocals on "Driving Down the Road in My Mind" and "Wishing."
R. Walt Vincent: harmony vocals on "Warren in the '60s" and "Quit That Scene."

Recorded at home by Tommy Keene
Drums recorded by Jonathan Pines, except drums on "Eyes of Youth" and "I've Heard That Wind Blow Before" recorded by Chris Widmer
Mixed by R. Walt Vincent at Studio Mesmer, Culver City, CA
"Warren in the Sixties" co-produced by R. Walt Vincent

1. "Black & White New York"
2. "Warren in the Sixties"
3. "Quit That Scene"
4. "Driving Down the Road in My Mind"
5. "Wishing"
6. "Lives Become Lies"
7. "Eyes of Youth"
8. "I've Heard That Wind Blow Before"
9. "Alta Loma"
10. "Texas Tower #4"

All songs written by Tommy Keene.

Singles

1983

"Back to Zero Now" b/w "Mr. Roland" (Avenue)
Produced by Tommy Keene and Ted Niceley.
Recorded by Steve Carr at Hit and Run Studios, Rockville, MD.
Both songs written by Tommy Keene.

1984

"Back Again (Try …) b/w "Safe in the Light"/"All I Want Is You"/"When the Whip Comes Down" (Dolphin)
"Back Again (Try …)" was recorded by T-Bone Burnett and Don Dixon at Reflection Sound Studios.
"Safe in the Light" was recorded by Steve Carr at Hit and Run Studios, Rockville, MD and remixed by Don Dixon and Steve Gronback at TGS Studios.
"All I Want Is You" and "When the Whip Comes Down" were recorded by Jim Crenca live at the Rat, Boston, MA on July 6, 1984.
"Back Again (Try …)" and "Safe in the Light" written by Tommy Keene, "All I Want Is You" written by Bryan Ferry, and "When the Whip Comes Down" written by Mick Jagger and Keith Richards.

1986

"Places That Are Gone" b/w "Faith in Love" (Geffen) [Canada]

"Places That Are Gone" is taken from the *Songs from the Film* album.

"Faith in Love" was produced by Tommy Keene and recorded by Steve Carr at Hit and Run Studios, Rockville, MD.

Both songs written by Tommy Keene.

"Listen to Me" b/w "Faith in Love" (Geffen)

"Listen to Me" is taken from the *Songs from the Film* album.

"Faith in Love" was produced by Tommy Keene and recorded by Steve Carr at Hit and Run Studios, Rockville, MD.

Both songs written by Tommy Keene.

Promotional Records

1986

"Places That Are Gone" (Geffen)

12" single with the song on both sides.

Taken from the *Songs from the Film* album.

Written by Tommy Keene.

"Listen to Me" b/w "Kill Your Sons" (Geffen)

12" single.

"Listen to Me" is taken from the *Songs from the Film* album.

"Kill Your Sons" was recorded live at the World in New York City on March 21, 1986. It was later released commercially on the *Run Now* EP.

"Listen to Me" written by Tommy Keene and "Kill Your Sons" written by Lou Reed.

1989

"Based on Happy Times" b/w "Our Car Club" (Geffen)

12" single.

Both songs are taken from the *Based on Happy Times* album.

"Based on Happy Times" written by Tommy Keene and "Our Car Club" written by Brian Wilson and Mike Love.

"Our Car Club" (Geffen)
  CD single.
  Taken from the *Based on Happy Times* album.
  Written by Brian Wilson and Mike Love.

Various Artist Compilation and Soundtrack Albums

1981

Connected (Limp)
  Sampler album of acts from the Washington, D.C. area. Includes "Strange Alliance" and "The Heart (Is a Lonely Place to Hide)" by Tommy Keene.

1986

Out of Bounds (IRS)
  Soundtrack album. Includes "Run Now" by Tommy Keene. Keene and his band also make a brief appearance in the movie.

1993

Yellow Pills: The Best of American Pop, vol. 1 (Big Deal)
  Power pop compilation. Includes "Disarray" by Tommy Keene.

1995

sing HOLLIES in reverse (eggBERT)
  Hollies tribute album. Includes Tommy Keene's cover of "Carrie Anne."

1997

Poptopia!: Power Pop Classics of the '80s (Rhino)
  Power pop compilation. Includes the Geffen version of "Places That Are Gone."

The Bucketfull of Brains 50th Anniversary CD
  Compilation album included with issue #50 of the zine *Bucketfull of Brains*. Includes "There's No One in This City" by Tommy Keene.

2006

The Who Covered

Compilation album that contains Who songs covered by various artists and came with the February 2006 issue of the British rock magazine *Mojo*. Includes Tommy Keene's version of "Tattoo."

Pop Culture Press Spring + Summer 2006 CD Sampler 24
CD sampler included with issue #62 of *Pop Culture Press*. Includes "Black & White New York" by Tommy Keene.

With Razz

(Note: Razz released one single, "C. Redux" b/w "70's Anomie" (O'Rourke), in 1977, before Tommy Keene joined the band.)

EP

1979

Air Time (O'Rourke)

> Michael Reidy: vocals
> Tommy Keene: guitar and vocals
> Bill Craig: guitar
> Ted Niceley: bass
> Doug Tull: drums

Recorded on November 3, 1978 at the Student Union Grand Ballroom at the University of Maryland, College Park, MD.
Edited by Skip Groff.

Side One:
1. "Marianne"
2. "Cherry Vanilla"

Side Two:
3. "Love Is Love"
4. "Hippy Hippy Shake"

"Marianne" and "Love Is Love" written by Miachael Reidy and Tommy Keene, "Cherry Vanilla" written by Michael Reidy and Abaad Behram, and "Hippy Hippy Shake" written by Chan Romero.

Single

1979

"You Can Run" b/w "Who's Mr. Comedy" (O'Rourke)
Both songs written by Michael Reidy and Tommy Keene.

With the Keene Brothers

2006

Blues and Boogie Shoes

Robert Pollard: lead vocals.
Tommy Keene: guitar, bass, keyboards, and harmony vocals.
John Richardson: drums on "Where Other Fail," "The Naked Wall," "You Must Engage," "This Time Do You Feel It?," and "A Blue Shadow."
Jon Wurster: drums on "Evil vs. Evil," "Beauty of the Draft," and "Heaven's Gate."
R. Walt Vincent: piano on "Death of the Party" and harmony vocals.

Drums on "Where Other Fail," "You Must Engage," and "A Blue Shadow" recorded by Jonathan Pines, drums on "Evil vs. Evil," "Beauty of the Draft," and "Heaven's Gate" recorded by R. Walt Vincent, and drums on "The Naked Wall" and "This Time Do You Feel It?" recorded by Chris Widmer.
Robert Pollard's vocals recorded by Todd Tobias at Waterloo Sound, Kent, OH.
Most everything else recorded by Tommy Keene at home.
"Evil vs. Evil," "Beauty of the Draft," "Where Other Fail," "Island of Lost Lucys," "Heaven's Gate," "The Camouflaged Friend," "You Must Engage," and "A Blue Shadow" mixed by Jonathan Pines at Private Studios, Urbana, IL.
"Death of the Party," "Lost Upon Us," "The Naked Wall," and "This Time Do You Feel It?" mixed by R. Walt Vincent at Studio Mesmer, Culver City, CA.

1. "Evil vs. Evil"
2. "Death of the Party"
3. "Beauty of the Draft"
4. "Where Other Fail"
5. "Island of Lost Lucys"
6. "Lost Upon Us"
7. "Heaven's Gate"
8. "The Naked Wall"
9. "The Camouflaged Friend"
10. "You Must Engage"
11. "This Time Do You Feel It?"
12. "A Blue Shadow"

All songs written by Robert Pollard and Tommy Keene.

As Producer

1987

***Waiting for No One* by Carnival Season** (What Goes On)
Album produced by Tommy Keene. Brad Quinn played bass in this band.

1989

***Yes Ma'am* by Satellite Boyfriend** (Stew)
Tommy Keene produced two songs on the album, "Scared at 19" and "Alicia in the Black Dress" and played guitar on "Alicia in the Black Dress."

As Sideman

1982

"(Meet the) Flinstones" b/w "Take Me Out to the Ballgame" by Bruce Springstone (Clean Cuts)
Bruce Springsteen parody. Tommy Keene plays guitar.

1993

***Illiterature* by Adam Schmitt** (Reprise)

Tommy Keene plays a guitar solo on "Three Faces West." Jay Bennett, Brad Quinn, and John Richardson also appear on various cuts on the album.

1998

Dizzy Up the Girl by the Goo Goo Dolls (Warner Bros.)
Tommy Keene plays guitar on "Broadway."

2000

Rock Concert by Velvet Crush (Action Musik)
Recorded live at the Cabaret Metro in Chicago in March 1995. With Tommy Keene on guitar and harmony vocals.

2002

Tunes Young People Will Enjoy by Jesse Valenzuela
Tommy Keene plays guitar on one track.

2006

Moon by Robert Pollard and the Ascended Masters (Merge)
Recorded live at the U.S. Bank Arena in Cincinnati, OH on June 24, 2006. With Tommy Keene on guitar and keyboards. Given away as a bonus disc with Robert Pollard's *Normal Happiness* album.

IV. Gig List

Thanks to Dave Franco, George Makovic, Troy Paterson, and Fabien Petit for their contributions to this list.

While this is the most comprehensive gig list that I have been able to compile to date, there are still some gaps at this point. Any additional information for future editions of this book would be greatly appreciated and may be sent to rockbeat@starpower.net.

1981

August 18, The Door, Washington, DC
Opening for the Flaming Ohs. In addition to Tommy Keene, the Tommy Keene Group at this time consisted of Ted Niceley on bass, Doug Tull on drums, and Michael Colburn on guitar. Colburn subsequently left the band and was replaced by Billy Connelly.

September 12, Desperado's, Washington, DC

October 2, The Marble Bar, Baltimore, MD

October 7, The Bayou, Washington, DC
Opening for Icehouse.

October 29, Desperado's, Washington, DC

November 11, The 9:30 Club, Washington, DC
Opening for Tom Verlaine.

November 20, The Psychedelly, Bethesda, MD

December 4, Desperado's, Washington, DC

December 10, The Bayou, Washington, DC
Opening for the Romantics.

December 13, The 9:30 Club, Washington, DC
This was a record release party to celebrate the release of the *Connected* album by Limp Records. *Connected* was a sampler album of acts from the Washingon, DC area, which was assembled by Skip Groff of Yesterday and Today Records. The album included two tracks by Tommy Keene, "Strange Alliance" and "The Heart (Is a Lonely Place to Hide)". The bill for this show also included Black Maket Baby, Nightman, the Slickee Boys, and the Velvet Monkeys.

1982

January 7, The 9:30 Club, Washington, DC
On a bill with Dirty Looks.

January 13, Trax, New York, NY
On a bill with the Pedestrians.

May 7, The Marble Bar, Baltimore, MD

May 14, Ritchie Coliseum, University of Maryland, College Park, MD
Opening for the Jam.

May 28, The 9:30 Club, Washington, DC

June 14, The Bayou, Washington, DC

June 28, The Wax Museum, Washington, DC
Opening for the Motels.

July 27, The Ritz, New York, NY

August 4, The Wax Museum, Washington, DC
Opening for David Johansen.

August 27, The 9:30 Club, Washington, DC

September 24, The Wax Museum, Washington, DC

September 29, The Peppermint Lounge, New York, NY
Opening for Translator.

November 11, The 9:30 Club, Washington, DC

December 4, The Marble Bar, Baltimore, MD

December 7, The 9:30 Club, Washington, DC
This was a benefit show for *New York Rocker* magazine. The bill for the show also included the Slickee Boys, Underheaven, and Switchblade.

December 10, Warner Theater, Washington, DC
Opening for Marshall Crenshaw and Joe "King" Carrasco.

December 31, The 9:30 Club, Washington, DC
On a bill with the Slickee Boys.

1983

January 15, The Wax Museum, Washington, DC

March 5, The Marble Bar, Baltimore, MD

March 11, The 9:30 Club, Washington, DC

April 8, Friendship Station, Washington, DC

April 21, Civic Center, Baltimore, MD
Opening for the Stray Cats.

April 29, The Marble Bar, Baltimore, MD

May 3, The Bayou, Washington, DC

June 4, The Wax Museum, Washington, DC

June 11, The Danceteria, New York, NY
On a bill with the Slickee Boys and the Velvet Monkeys.

July 15, The 9:30 Club, Washington, DC

August 26, The 9:30 Club, Washington, DC

September 24, The Wax Museum, Washington, DC

October 6, The Wax Museum, Washington, DC
Opening for Graham Parker.

October 8, The Danceteria, New York, NY

October 27, Girard's, Baltimore, MD

November 11, The 9:30 Club, Washington, DC

December 8, Lisner Auditorium, Washington, DC
Opening for Marshall Crenshaw.

December 15, The Ritz, New York, NY
Opening for the Alarm.

1984

January 21, The 9:30 Club, Washington, DC

February 17, The Wax Museum, Washington, DC

March 30, The 9:30 Club, Washington, DC

April 12, The Psychedelly, Bethesda, MD

April 14, The Ritz, New York, NY
Opening for Modern English.

April 27, The Wax Museum, Washington, DC

Show opened by Abaad Behram's band, Johnny Bombay and the Reactions.

May 10 and 11, Savoy Theatre, New York, NY
Opening for the Style Council.

May 25, The 9:30 Club, Washington, DC

June 8, Saba Club, Washington, DC

June 9, Merriweather Post Pavillion, Columbia, MD
On a bill with the Ravyns.

July 3, The 9:30 Club, Washington, DC

July 6, The Rat, Boston, MA
The live versions of "All I Want Is You" and "When the Whip Comes Down" that appeared on the "Back Again (Try …)" 12" single were recorded at this show.

July 7, The Danceteria, New York, NY

July 9, The 8x10, Baltimore, MD

July 21, The 8x10, Baltimore, MD

July 27, Saba Club, Washington, DC

September 21, The Peppermint Lounge, New York, NY
On a bill with Green on Red.

October 20, Saba Club, Washington, DC

October 27, The 8x10, Baltimore, MD

November 10, The Psychedelly, Bethesda, MD

November 20, Saba Club, Washington, DC

November 21, The 9:30 Club, Washington, DC

November 23, Maxwell's, Hoboken, NJ

November 24, The Ritz, New York, NY
Opening for the Church. Alex Chilton was also on the bill, but canceled.

December 14, Saba Club, Washington, DC

December 28, The Psychedelly, Bethesda, MD

1985

January 18, The 9:30 Club, Washington, DC

January 30, The Paradise, Boston, MA
On a bill with Let's Active and Don Dixon.

February 1, Girard's, Baltimore, MD
On a bill with Let's Active and Don Dixon.

February 2, The Ritz, New York, NY
On a bill with Let's Active and Don Dixon.

February 7, Maxwell's, Hoboken, NJ

March 8, Grand Ballroom, Student Union, University of Maryland, College Park, MD
Opening for the Bongos.

March 15, The 9:30 Club, Washington, DC

March 22, The 8x10, Baltimore, MD

March 30, The Peppermint Lounge, New York, NY

April 3, 1985, Ontario Theatre, Washington, DC
On a bill with Aztec Camera and Guadalcanal Diary.

April 25, The 9:30 Club, Washington, DC

November 27, The 9:30 Club, Washington, DC

1986

March 4, The Roxy, Washington, DC
This was a warm-up gig for the *Songs from the Film* tour with Keene and band billed as the "Ted Niceley Experience." The gig helped to work in new drummer Rob Brill, who substituted on the tour for Doug Tull, who had thrown his back out the week before.

March 6, The Bayou, Washington, DC
Invitation-only record release party for industry types.

March 15, Godfrey's Famous Ballroom, Baltimore, MD
Opening night of *Songs from the Film* tour.

March 16, Cat's Cradle, Chapel Hill, NC

March 20, The Paradise, Boston, MA
The first of several shows opening for Lloyd Cole and the Commotions.

March 21, The World, New York, NY
Opening for Lloyd Cole and the Commotions. This show was filmed and broadcast on MTV. The live version of "Kill Your Sons" that appears on the *Run Now* EP is from this gig.
Set List:
1. "Astronomy"
2. "Nothing Can Change You"
3. "Gold Town"
4. "Places That Are Gone"
5. "Underworld"
6. "The Story Ends"
7. "Back to Zero Now"
8. "Listen to Me"
9. "As Life Goes By"

10. "Back Again"
Encore:
11. "Kill Your Sons"

March 24, The Spectrum, Montreal, Canada

March 25, The Copa, Toronto, Canada

March 28, St. Andrew's Ballroom, Detroit, MI

March 29, Park West, Chicago, IL

March 30, First Avenue & 7th Street Entry, Minneapolis, MN

April 1, The Rainbow Theatre, Denver, CO

April 2, The Palladium, Salt Lake City, UT

April 4, Wolfgang's, San Francisco, CA

April 6, The Palace, Los Angeles, CA

April 7, San Diego State University, San Diego, CA

April 13, One Step Beyond, Santa Clara, CA

April 15, Starry Night, Portland, OR

April 16 and 17, Backstage, Seattle, WA

April 19, WBCN Expo, Boston, MA

April 27, The 9:30 Club, Washington, DC

July 29, Kings Head Inn, Norfolk, VA
Doug Tull returns on drums.

July 31, Rockitz, Richmond, VA

August 1, The 9:30 Club, Washington, DC

August 14, The Ritz, New York, NY
Opening for Icehouse.

August 15, Maxwell's Hoboken, NJ

August 16, The Rat, Boston, MA

August 30, George Washington University, Washington, DC

September 26, University of Richmond, Richmond, VA

October 6, Glassboro State College, NJ
Opening for Southside Johnny and the Asbury Jukes.

October 17, Haverford, PA

November 1, Utica College, NY

Opening night of the *Run Now* tour. Opening for Til Tuesday.

November 2, Hamilton College, Clinton, NY

November 5, Blind Pig, Ann Arbor, MI

November 7, Century Hall, Milwaukee, WI
On a bill with the Dead Milkmen.

November 8, O'Cayze Corral, Madison, WI

November 9, First Avenue & 7th Street Entry, Minneapolis, MN
On a bill with Hunters and Collectors. Paul Westerberg in attendance.

November 10, Blue Note, Columbia, MO

November 12, Cogburn's, Lawrence, KS

November 13, Mississippi Nights, St. Louis, MO

November 15, Rivera Theatre, Chicago, IL
On a bill with Steve Earle.

November 16, Mabel's, Champaign, IL
Show opened by Pop the Balloon, which included Adam Schmitt and Ric Menck.

November 17, Columbus, OH

November 19, The Bayou, Washington, DC

November 21, The 8x10, Baltimore, MD

November 23, Kings Head Inn, Norfolk, VA

December 2, The Brewery, Raleigh, NC

December 3, Rockefeller's, Columbia, SC

December 4, Milestone, Charlotte, NC

December 5, Uptown Lounge, Athens, GA

December 6, The Nick, Birmingham, AL

December 7, Exit Inn, Nashville, TN

December 9, Lucky's, Radford, VA

December 11, Spit, Boston, MA

December 12, The Grotto, New Haven, CT

December 13, City Gardens, Trenton, NJ

1987

April 30, The Bayou, Washington, DC
  With an unknown drummer replacing Doug Tull.

May 1, Maxwell's, Hoboken, NJ

May 2, The 8x10, Baltimore, MD

May 4, J.C. Dobbs, Philadelphia, PA

May 5, Club Metro, Virginia Beach, VA

May 6, Kingshead Inn, Norfolk, VA

May 7, Lucky's, Radford, VA

May 8, Hampden, Sidney College, VA

October 28, Constitution Hall, Washington, DC
  Solo, opening for Suzanne Vega.

November 25, Shriver Hall, Johns Hopkins University, Baltimore, MD
Solo, opening for Marti Jones and Don Dixon.

December 3, Lynchburg College, Lynchburg, VA
Solo.

December 4, Washington & Lee University, Lexington, VA
Solo.

December 9, Pterodactyl, Charlotte, NC
Solo.

December 10, Uptown Lounge, Athens, GA
Solo.

December 11, Beatty's, Winston-Salem, NC
Solo.

December 12, The 8x10, Baltimore, MD
Solo, opening for Alex Chilton.

1988

No known gigs.

1989

March 30, Maxwell's, Hoboken, NJ
Opening night of the *Based on Happy Times* tour. Debut of the new band featuring Justin Hibbard on guitar, Brad Quinn (formerly of Carnival Season) on bass, and John Richardson on drums.

March 31, 7 Willow Street, Port Chester, NY

April 1, Krypton, Banksville, NY

April 2, The Chance, Poughkeepsie, NY

April 4, Nightstage, Cambridge, MA

April 5, Hammerjack's, Baltimore, MD

April 6, The Warner Theater, Washington, DC
Opening for the Replacements.

April 7, Tower Theater, Philadelphia, PA
Opening for the Replacements.
Set List:
1. "This Could Be Fiction"
2. "Nothing Can Change You"
3. "Hanging on to Yesterday"
4, "Light of Love"
5. "Based on Happy Times"
6. "Back to Zero Now"
7. "Listen to Me"
8. "When Our Vows Break"
9. "My Mother Looked Like Marilyn Monroe"
10. "Places That Are Gone"

April 8, Downtown Club, New York, NY

April 10, The Boat House, Norfolk, VA
Opening for the Replacements.

April 11, The Mosque, Richmond, VA
Opening for the Replacements.

April 12, The Speakeasy, Raleigh, NC
Opening for the Replacements.

April 13, 1313, Charlotte, NC
Opening for the Replacements.

April 14, Center Stage, Atlanta, GA
Opening for the Replacements.

April 15, Janus Landing, St. Petersburg, FL
Opening for the Replacements.
Set List:
1. "Nothing Can Change You"
2. "Astronomy"
3. "This Could Be Fiction"
4. "Hanging on to Yesterday"
5. "Light of Love"
6. "Back to Zero Now"
7. "Hey Man"
8. "When Our Vows Break"
9. "My Mother Looked Like Marilyn Monroe"
10. "Places That Are Gone"
11. "Shake Some Action"

April 17, Cameo Theater, Miami, FL
Opening for the Replacements.

April 18, Beacham Theater, Orlando, FL
Opening for the Replacements.

April 19, Emory University, Atlanta, GA
Opening for the Replacements.

April 20, Sloss Furnace, Birmingham, AL
Opening for the Replacements.

April 21, Antenna Club, Memphis, TN

April 22, The Cannery, Nashville, TN

April 24, Uptown Lounge, Athens, GA

April 25, Greenstreets, Columbia, SC

April 26, Orchestra Pit, Winston-Salem, NC

April 27, The Brewery, Raleigh, NC

April 28, The 9:30 Club, Washington, DC
Robyn Hitchcock made an unannounced appearance as part of a promotional tour, and performed a brief acoustic set prior to Keene's set.
Set List:
1. "Alive"
2. "Nothing Can Change You"
3. "Astronomy"
4. "This Could Be Fiction"
5. "Paper Words and Lies"
6. "Hanging on to Yesterday"
7. "Light of Love"
8. "No One in this City"
9. "Back to Zero Now"
10. "Based on Happy Times"
11. "Listen to Me"
12. "Run Now"
13. "When Our Vows Break"
14. "My Mother Looked Like Marilyn Monroe"
15. "Places That Are Gone"
First Encore:
16. "Our Car Club"
17. "Shake Some Action"
18. "In the Street"
Second Encore:
19. "Kill Your Sons"

April 29, The 9:30 Club, Washington, DC
Set List:
1. "Alive"
2. "Nothing Can Change You"
3. "Astronomy"
4. "This Could Be Fiction"
5. "Hanging on to Yesterday"
6. "Light of Love"
7. "No One in this City"
8. "Back to Zero Now"

9. "Based on Happy Times"
10. "Listen to Me"
11. "Run Now"
12. "When Our Vows Break"
13. "My Mother Looked Like Marilyn Monroe"
14. "Places That Are Gone"
First Encore:
15. "Our Car Club"
16. "Shake Some Action"
17. "In the Street"
Second Encore:
18. "Nighttime" (solo)
19. "Faith in Love" (solo)
20. "Kill Your Sons"

June 30, The 9:30 Club, Washington, DC
A brief, unadvertised set used to shake down new material prior to going into Hit and Run Studios to record demos. Keene appeared between the opening act, Carnival of Souls, and the headliner, Radio Blue.
Set List:
1. "In the Street"
2. "Something to Rave About"
3. "Soul Searching"
4. "No One in this City"
5. "Hey Man"
6. "Alive"
7. "Waiting to Fly"
8. "Driving into the Sun"
9. "Compromise"
10. "Crack City"
Encore:
11. "Shake Some Action"

July 1, The Green Parrot, Neptune, NJ

July 6, Max's on Broadway, Baltimore, MD

July 7, The 9:30 Club, Washington, DC

July 8, The 9:30 Club, Washington, DC

1990

March 22, The 8x10, Baltimore, MD

With Eric Peterson (formerly of the dBs) taking over the second guitar slot.

Set List:

1. "Alive"
2. "Nothing Can Change You"
3. "Astronomy"
4. "This Could Be Fiction"
5. "Hanging on to Yesterday"
6. "Down, Down, Down"
7. "Driving into the Sun"
8. "Hey Man"
9. "Soul Searching"
10. "Good Thing Going"
11. "Run Now"
12. "Compromise"
13. "When Our Vows Break"
14. "My Mother Looked Like Marilyn Monroe"
15. "Places That Are Gone"

First Encore:

16.? (Then-unreleased new song) (solo acoustic)
17. "Back to Zero Now" (solo acoustic)
18. "Our Car Club"

Second Encore:

19. "Shake Some Action"

March 23, Metro, Richmond, VA

March 24, Cat's Cradle, Chapel Hill, NC

March 28, CBGB, New York, NY

March 30, The 9:30 Club, Washington, DC

Show opened by Satellite Boyfriend. Keene produced a couple of songs on Satellite Boyfriend's album, *Yes Ma'am*, which was released on the Stew label in 1989.

Set List:

1. "Alive"
2. "Nothing Can Change You"
3. "Astronomy"
4. "This Could Be Fiction"
5. "Hanging on to Yesterday"
6. "Down, Down, Down"
7. "Hey Man"
8. "Soul Searching"
9. "Run Now"
10. "Good Thing Going"
11. "Love Is a Dangerous Thing"
12. "When Our Vows Break"
13. "Compromise"
14. "My Mother Looked Like Marilyn Monroe"
15. "Places That Are Gone"

First Encore:

16. ? (Then-unreleased new song) (solo acoustic)
17. "That's When I Reach for My Revolver" (solo acoustic)
18. "Back to Zero Now" (solo acoustic)
19. "Our Car Club"
Second Encore:
20. "Shake Some Action"
21. "Kill Your Sons"
Third Encore:
22. "In the Street"
23. "Route 66"

March 31, Peabody's, Virginia Beach, VA

June 30, Gaston Hall, Georgetown University, Washington, DC
Solo, opening for Marti Jones and Don Dixon.
Set List:
1. "Hey Man"
2. "Time"
3. "Babyface"
4. ? (Then-unreleased new song)
5. "My Mother Looked Like Marilyn Monroe"
6. "Back to Zero Now"
7. "Down, Down, Down"
8. "I Don't Feel Right at All"
9. "Love Is a Dangerous Thing"
10. "Highwire Days"
11. "That's When I Reach for My Revolver"
12. "Mr. Roland"

September 15, The 9:30 Club, Washington, DC

December 8, The 9:30 Club, Washington, DC
Set List:
1. "Something to Rave About"
2. "Andrea"
3. "Call on Me"
4. "Your Heart Beats Alone"
5. "Hanging on to Yesterday"

6. "Alive"
7. "Astronomy"
8. "This Could Be Fiction"
9. "Down, Down, Down"
10. "Hey Man"
11. "Soul Searching"
12. "Gold Town"
13. "My Mother Looked Like Marilyn Monroe"
14. "When Our Vows Break"
15. "Good Thing Going"
16. "Love Is a Dangerous Thing"
Encore:
17. "Baby Strange"
18. "Places That Are Gone"
19. "Kill Your Sons"
20. "Nothing Can Change You"
21. "Our Car Club"

December 18, The Birchmere, Alexandria, VA
Solo.

1991

June?, The Point, Atlanta, GA

June 16, City Stages Festival, Birmingham, AL
Set List:
1. "Alive"
2. "Astronomy"
3. "This Could Be Fiction"
4. "We Started Over Again"
5. "Hanging on to Yesterday"
6. "Back to Zero Now"
7. "Hey Man"
8. "Andrea"
9. "Call on Me"
10. "When Our Vows Break"
11. "My Mother Looked Like Marilyn Monroe"

12. "Places That Are Gone"

June 29, The 9:30 Club, Washington, DC

June 30, The 8x10, Baltimore, MD

1992

September 19, Cabaret Metro, Chicago, IL
Opening for the Connells.

September 26, Hammerjack's, Baltimore, MD
Opening for the Connells.

October 6, The Masquerade, Atlanta, GA
Set List:
1. "Alive"
2. "Astronomy"
3. "This Could Be Fiction"
4. "Nothing Can Change You"
5. "Hanging on to Yesterday"
6. "Down, Down, Down"
7. "We Started Over Again"
8. "Compromise"
9. "When our Vows Break"
10. "Love Is a Dangerous Thing"
11. "My Mother Looked Like Marilyn Monroe"
12. "Places That Are Gone"

October 9, The 8x10, Baltimore, MD

October 10, The 9:30 Club, Washington, DC

1993

March 13, Cabaret Metro, Chicago, IL

March 14, Beat Kitchen, Chicago, IL

March 21, The 8x10, Baltimore, MD

March 24, The 9:30 Club, Washington, DC

May 16, Bottom of the Hill, San Francisco, CA
Set List:
1. "Alive"
2. "Astronomy"
3. "Down, Down, Down"
4. "Back to Zero Now"
5. "Compromise"
6. "When Our Vows Break"
7. "Good Thing Going"
8. "My Mother Looked Like Marilyn Monroe"
9. "Love Is a Dangerous Thing"
10. "Places That Are Gone"
Encore:
11. "In the Street"

1994

February 1, The Late Show with Conan O'Brien, New York, NY
Keene and band performed "Places That Are Gone" and Keene chatted briefly with O'Brien.

February 2, Wetlands, New York, NY

February 3, Causeway, Boston, MA

February 4, The Fastlane, Asbury Park, NJ

February 5, The 9:30 Club, Washington, DC

February 6, JC Dobb's, Philadelphia, PA

February 7, Club Z, Harrisburg, PA

February 9, Cicero's, St. Louis, MO

February 10, Gabe's Oasis, Iowa City, IA

February 11, Cubby Bear, Chicago, IL

February 12, Brett's, Milwaukee, WI

February 13, Uptown, Minneapolis, MN

March 19, University of Missouri, Rolla, MO
Opening for the Gin Blossoms.

March 20, University of Illinois, Champaign, IL
Opening for the Gin Blossoms.

March 21, Northern Illinois University, Dekalb, IL
Opening for the Gin Blossoms.

March 22, Memorial Gym, Quincy, IL
Opening for the Gin Blossoms.

March 24, University of Wisconsin, Stevens Point, WI
Opening for the Gin Blossoms.

March 25, Augustana College, Davenport, IA
Opening for the Gin Blossoms.

March 26, University of Notre Dame, South Bend, IN
Opening for the Gin Blossoms.

March 28, University of Wisconsin, LaCrosse, WI
Opening for the Gin Blossoms.

March 29, University of Wisconsin, Platteville, WI
Opening for the Gin Blossoms.

March 30, Ripon College, Ripon, WI

Opening for the Gin Blossoms.

April 1, Second Avenue, Indianapolis, IN
Opening for the Gin Blossoms.

April 2, Newport Music Hall, Columbus, OH
Opening for the Gin Blossoms.

April 4, Muskingum College, New Concord, OH
Opening for the Gin Blossoms.

April 5, Ohio University, Athens, OH
Opening for the Gin Blossoms.

April 6, Duquesne University, Pittsburgh, PA
Opening for the Gin Blossoms.

April 12, Rowan College, Glassboro, NJ
Opening for the Gin Blossoms.

April 13, Fisher Auditorium, Indiana, PA
Opening for the Gin Blossoms.

April 15, Sacred Heart University, Fairfield, CT
Opening for the Gin Blossoms.

April 16, Providence College, Providence, RI
Opening for the Gin Blossms.

April 17, Cornell University, Ithaca, NY
Opening for the Gin Blossoms.

April 18, Lee's Place, Toronto, Ontario
Opening for the Gin Blossoms.

April 20, Albright College, Reading, PA
Opening for the Gin Blossoms.

April 21, University of Scranton, Scranton, PA
Opening for the Gin Blossoms.

April 22, Lycomning College, Williamsport, PA
Opening for the Gin Blossoms.

April 23, University of Rochester, Rochester, NY
Opening for the Gin Blossoms.

April 24, SUNY Oneonta, Oneanta, NY
Opening for the Gin Blossoms.

1995

December 23, The 9:30 Club, Washington, DC
One of a series of shows commemorating the 9:30 Club's final days at its original location at 9:30 F Street, NW.
Set List:
1. (Inaudible due to sound problems)
2. "This Could Be Fiction"

3. "Turning on Blue"
4. "Paper Words and Lies"
5. "Down, Down, Down"
6. "Nothing Can Change You"
7. "On the Runway"
8. "Astronomy"
9. "Your Heart Beats Alone"
10. "Alive"
11. "Silent Town"
12. "Back to Zero Now"
13. "Good Thing Going"
14. "Compromise"
15. "Love Is a Dangerous Thing"
First Encore:
16. "Our Car Club"
17. "Hey! Little Child"
18. "Kill Your Sons"
19. "In the Street"
Second Encore:
20. "Places That Are Gone"

1996

March 18, Duquesne University, Pittsburgh, PA
Opening for the Gin Blossoms.

March 20, Harris East Theatre, Rochester, NY
Opening for the Gin Blossoms.

March 25, Catholic University, Washington, DC
Opening for the Gin Blossoms.

March 27, St. Joseph's College, Philadelphia, PA
Opening for the Gin Blossoms.

March 28, York College, York, PA
Opening for the Gin Blossoms.

March 29, Iona College, New Rochelle, NY
Opening for the Gin Blossoms

April?, Cabaret Metro, Chicago, IL

April 21, Furman University, Greeneville, SC
Opening for the Gin Blossoms.

April 22, University of North Carolina, Chapel Hill, NC
Opening for the Gin Blossoms.

April 23, Daniel Recital Hall, Greeneville, SC
Opening for the Gin Blossoms.

April 24, Campbell University, Buie's Creek, NC
Opening for the Gin Blossoms.

April 25, University of Delaware, Newark, DE
Opening for the Gin Blossoms.

April 26, Reitz Arena, Loyola College, Baltimore, MD
Opening for the Gin Blossoms.

April 28, Slippery Rock University, Slippery Rock, PA
Opening for the Gin Blossoms.

April 29, Franklin & Marshall College, Lancaster, PA
Opening for the Gin Blossoms.

April 30, The 9:30 Club, Washington, DC
Opening for Modern English.
Set List:
1. "Call on Me"
2. "Going Out Again"
3. "Turning on Blue"
4. "Nothing Can Change You"
5. "Silent Town"
6. "Compromise"

7. "Love Is a Dangerous Thing"
8. "Our Car Club"
Encore:
9. "In the Street"

May 1, Pace University, Pleasantville, PA
Opening for the Gin Blossoms.

May 2, Assumption College, Worcester, MA
Opening for the Gin Blossoms.

May 3, Rochester Institute of Technology, Rochester, NY
Opening for the Gin Blossoms.

May 4, SUNY Buffalo, Bauffalo, NY
Opening for the Gin Blossoms.

May 6, Concert Hall, Toronto, Ontario
Opening for the Gin Blossoms.

May 7, Barrymores, Ottawa, Ontario
Opening for the Gin Blossoms.

May 8, Spectrum, Montreal, Quebec
Opening for the Gin Blossoms.

May 10, Rockland Community College, Suffern, NY
Opening for the Gin Blossoms.

May 11, Western Connecticut University, Danbury, CT
Opening for the Gin Blossoms.

1997

No known gigs.

1998

March 18, Liberty Lunch, Austin, TX
Appearance at the SXSW Festival.

May 6, Cicero's, St. Louis, MO
With Scott Johnson (of the Gin Blossoms) taking over the second guitar slot.

May 7, Schuba's, Chicago, IL
Set List:
1. "Call on Me"
2. "Battle Lines"
3. "Going Out Again"
4. "Long Time Missing"
5. "Silent Town"
6. "Einstein's Day"
7. "Nothing Can Change You"
8. "Waiting Without You"
9. "Paper Words and Lies"
10. "Getting Out from Under You"
11. "Underworld"
12. "Back to Zero Now"
13. "When Our Vows Break"
14. "Compromise"
15. "Love Is a Dangerous Thing"
Encore:
16. "Based on Happy Times"
17. "Highwire Days"
18. "Places That Are Gone"
19. "Kill Your Sons"

May 8, First Avenue & 7th Street Entry, Minneapolis, MN

May 9, Cactus Bar, Milwaukee, WI
Set List:
1. "Battle Lines"
2. "Going Out Again"
3. "Long Time Missing"

4. "Silent Town"
5. "Einstein's Day"
6. "Astronomy"
7. "Nothing Can Change You"
8. "Waiting Without You"
9. "Paper Words and Lies"
10. "Getting Out from Under You"/"The World Outside"
11. "Underworld"
12. "When Our Vows Break"
13. "My Mother Looked Like Marilyn Monroe"
14. "Compromise"
15. "Love Is a Dangerous Thing"
Encore:
16. "Back to Zero Now"
17. "Places That Are Gone"

May 11, Lynagh's, Lexington, KY

May 13, TT the Bear's, Cambridge, MA

May 14, Brownie's, New York, NY

May 15, The 9:30 Club, Washington, DC
Keene played a brief set prior to a big, radio station-sponsored show that featured Semisonic, Grant Lee Buffalo, Daniel Lanois with Emmylou Harris, and Scott Weiland.
Set List:
1. "Battle Lines"
2. "Going Out Again"
3. "Long Time Missing"
4. "Silent Town"
5. "Astronomy"
6. "Nothing Can Change You"
7. "Compromise"
8. "Places That Are Gone"

May 16, Pontiac Grill, Philadelphia, PA

May 17, The Grogshop, Cleveland, OH

May 28, KCRW, Santa Monica, CA
In-studio interview and performance.
Set List:
1. "Astronomy"
2. "Waiting Without You"
3. "Long Time Missing"
4. "When Our Vows Break"
5. "Compromise"
6. "Love Is a Dangerous Thing"

May 28, The Troubadour, Los Angeles, CA

May 29, The Peacock Lounge, San Francisco, CA

May 30, Brick by Brick, San Diego, CA

July 29, Schuba's, Chicago, IL
With Steve Gerlach (formerly of the Phantom Helmsmen) taking over the second guitar slot.
Set List:
1. "Call on Me"
2. "Battle Lines"
3. "Going Out Again"
4. "Long Time Missing"
5. "Silent Town"
6. "Einstein's Day"
7. "Waiting Without You"
8. "Paper Words and Lies"
9. "Getting Out from under You"
10. "Underworld"
11. "Back to Zero Now"
12. "When Our Vows Break"
13. "Compromise"
14. "Love Is a Dangerous Thing"
First Encore:
15. "Based on Happy Times"

16. "Highwire Days"
17. "Places That Are Gone"
Second Encore:
18. "Kill Your Sons"

July 31, The Iota, Arlington, VA

Set List:
1. "Call on Me"
2. "Battle Lines"
3. "Going Out Again"
4. "Long Time Missing"
5. "Silent Town"
6. "Einstein's Day"
7. "Astronomy"
8. "Nothing Can Change You"
9. "Waiting Without You"
10. "Paper Words and Lies"
11. "Underworld"
12. "Highwire Days"
13. "When Our Vows Break"
14. "Compromise"
15. "Love Is a Dangerous Thing"
First Encore:
16. "Never Really Been Gone" (solo)
17. "Mary Anne with the Shaky Hand" (solo)
18. "Based on Happy Times"
19. "Back to Zero Now"
Second Encore:
20. "Places That Are Gone"
21. "Kill Your Sons"

August 1, The Iota, Arlington, VA

Set List:
1. "Never Really Been Gone" (solo)
2. "Silent Town"
3. "Call on Me"
4. "Going Out Again"
5. "Long Time Missing"

6. "Battle Lines"
7. "Einstein's Day"
8. "Astronomy"
9. "Nothing Can Change You"
10. "Waiting Without You"
11. "Paper Words and Lies"
12. "Getting Out from Under You"
13. "Underworld"
14. "Highwire Days"
15. "When Our Vows Break"
16. "Compromise"
17. "Love Is a Dangerous Thing"
First Encore:
18. "Based on Happy Times"
19. "Back to Zero Now"
20. "Places That Are Gone"
Second Encore:
21. "Kill Your Sons"

November 24–28 and December 1–5, The Chesterfield Cafe, Paris, France
Brad Jones substituted on bass for this series of shows.
Set List for November 27:
1. "Never Really Been Gone" (solo)
2. "Silent Town"
3. "When Our Vows Break"
4. "Long Time Missing"
5. "Astronomy"
6. "Getting Out from Under You"
7.? (solo)
8. "Waiting Without You"
9. "Safe in the Light"
10. "Going Out Again"
11. "Back to Zero Now"
12. "Compromise"
13. "Places That Are Gone"

1999

No known gigs.

2000

February 16, Irish Rover, Salamanca, Spain

February 17, La Casa Del Loco, Zaragoza, Spain

February 18, Bilborrock, Bilbao, Spain

February 19, Camelot Club, Santa Pola, Spain

February 20, Castellon De la Plana, Spain

February 22, Moby Dick Club, Madrid, Spain

February 23, Cadiz University, Spain

February 24, Salamadra Club, Sevilla, Spain

February 25, Sonotone, Marrorca, Spain

February 26, The Black Note, Valancia, Spain

February 29, The Double Door, Chicago, IL
    Set List:
    1. "Astronomy"
    2. "This Could Be Fiction"
    3. "On the Runway"
    4. "The Man Without a Soul"
    5. "Paper Words and Lies"
    6. "Long Time Missing"
    7. "Einstein's Day"
    8. "Silent Town"
    9. "Highwire Days"
    10. "Going Out Again"

11. "Safe in the Light"
12. "When Our Vows Break"
13. "Back to Zero Now"
14. "Compromise"
15. "Love Is a Dangerous Thing"
16. "Begin Where We End"
First Encore:
17. "Turning on Blue"
18. "Hey! Little Child"
19. "Places That Are Gone"
Second Encore:
20. "Shake Some Action"
21. "Kill Your Sons"

June 20, Ramshead Tavern, Annapolis, MD

June 21, Mercury Lounge, New York, NY

June 22, Upstage, Philadelphia, PA

June 23, The Iota, Arlington, VA

June 24, The Iota, Arlington, VA
Set List:
1. "Astronomy"
2. "This Could Be Fiction"
3. "On the Runway"
4. "The Man Without a Soul"
5. "Paper Words and Lies"
6. "Long Time Missing"
7. "Big Blue Sky"
8. "Places That Are Gone"
9. "Silent Town"
10. "Highwire Days"
11. "Going Out Again"
12. "Safe in the Light"
13. "Compromise"
14. "Love Is a Dangerous Thing"

15.? (Then-unreleased new song)
First Encore:
16. "Back to Zero Now"
17. "Underworld"
18. "All Your Love Will Stay"
Second Encore:
19. "Shake Some Action"
20. "Kill Your Sons"

2001

No known gigs.

2002

August 15, Nita's Hideaway, Tempe, AZ

August 17, The Bottom of the Hill, San Francisco, CA

August 19, The Troubadour, Los Angeles, CA

August 22, North Star Bar, Philadelphia, PA

August 23, The Iota, Arlington, VA
  Set List:
  1. "Begin Where We End"
  2. "Long Time Missing"
  3. "The Man Without a Soul"
  4. "Down, Down, Down"
  5. "Hanging Over My Head"
  6. "Nothing Can Change You"
  7. "The Biggest Conflict"
  8. "Big Blue Sky"
  9. "The Final Hour"
  10. "Silent Town"
  11. "Highwire Days"
  12. "My Mother Looked Like Marilyn Monroe"
  13. "Good Thing Going"

14. "Circumstance"
15. "Turning on Blue"
16. "Back to Zero Now"
17. "Compromise"
Encore:
18. "Astronomy"
19. "This Could Be Fiction"
20. "All Your Love Will Stay"
21. "Places That Are Gone"

August 24, The Iota, Arlington, VA
Solo, with guests.
Set List:
1. "Begin Where We End"
2. "Long Time Missing"
3. "Circumstance"
4. "Nighttime"
5. "Back Again"
6. "The Real Underground"
7. "Before the Lights Go Down"
8. "You Can't Wait for Time" (with Brad Quinn on bass)
9. "Back to Zero Now" (with Brad Quinn on bass and Billy Connelly on harmony vocals)
10. "Don't Sleep in the Daytime"
11. "On the Runway"
12. "Astronomy"
13. "The Story Ends"
14. "Safe in the Light" (with Steve Gerlach on guitar)
15. "If You're Getting Married Tonight" (with Steve Gerlach on guitar)
16. "Take Me Back" (with Steve Gerlach on guitar)
17. "Based on Happy Times" (with Steve Gerlach on guitar, Keene switches to electric guitar for the remainder of the set)
18. "Big Blue Sky"
19. "Highwire Days"
20. "That's When I Reach for My Revolver"
21. "Mr. Roland"
Encore:
22. "Call on Me"

23. "When Our Vows Break"
24. "Strange Alliance"
25. "Kill Your Sons"
(All encore numbers with Brad Quinn on bass, Steve Gerlach on guitar, and Mike Leach on drums.)

August 25, Mercury Lounge, New York, NY

August 26, TT the Bears, Cambridge, MA

August 28, Beachland Ballroom and Tavern, Cleveland, OH

August 29, Cactus Club, Milwaukee, WI

August 30, Schuba's Chicago, IL
Set List:
1. "Begin Where We End"
2. "Long Time Missing"
3. "The Man Without a Soul"
4. "Down, Down, Down"
5. "Hanging Over My Head"
6. "Nothing Can Change You"
7. "The Biggest Conflict"
8. "Big Blue Sky"
9. "The Final Hour"
10. "Underworld"
11. "Highwire Days"
12. "Places That Are Gone"

August 31, 400 Bar, Minneapolis, MN

October 25, Schuba's, Chicago, IL
Solo.
Set List:
1. "Begin Where We End"
2. "Long Time Missing"
3. "Circumstance"
4. "Nighttime"

5. "You Can't Wait for Time"
6. "When the Lights Go Down"
7. "Gold Town"
8. "Babyface"
9. "Astronomy"/"The Story Ends"
10. "Don't Sleep in the Daytime"
11. "Safe in the Light" (with Steve Gerlach on guitar)
12. "If You're Getting Married Tonight" (with Steve Gerlach on guitar)
13. "Take Me Back" (with Steve Gerlach on guitar)
14. "Based on Happy Times" (with Steve Gerlach on guitar)
Encore:
15. "Big Blue Sky"
16. "Highwire Days"
17. "Mr. Roland"
18. "That's When I Reach for My Revolver"
19. "Love Is a Dangerous Thing"

October 26, 400 Bar, Minneapolis, MN
Solo.

November 14, Crocodile Cafe, Seattle, WA
Solo.

November 15, Mt. Tabor Pub and Theatre, Portland, OR
Solo.

November 17, Cafe Du Nord, San Francisco, CA
Solo.

November 19, The Mint, Los Angeles, CA
Solo.

2003

March 27, 2003, The Knitting Factory, Los Angeles, CA

August 20, Bimbo's 365, San Francisco, CA
Opening for Guided by Voices.

August 22, Spaceland, Los Angeles, CA
Opening for Guided by Voices.

September 6, The Iota, Arlington, VA
Set List:
1. "Call on Me"
2. "Long Time Missing"
3. "When Our Vows Break"
4. "Down, Down, Down"
5. "The Man Without a Soul"
6. "Hanging Over My Head"
7. "Nothing Can Change You"
8. "The Biggest Conflict"
9. "Paper Words and Lies"
10. "Silent Town"
11. "Underworld"
12. "Turning on Blue"
13. "Back to Zero Now"
14. "Places That Are Gone"
15. "Begin Where We End"
First Encore:
16. "Highwire Days"
17. "Compromise"
18. "Love Is a Dangerous Thing"
19. "Strange Alliance"
Second Encore:
20. "Hey! Little Child"
21. "Kill Your Sons"

September 7, private wedding reception

2004

September 9, The Paradise, Boston, MA
Mike Leach substituted on drums for this series of shows. Opening for Guided by Voices.
Set List:

1. "Call on Me"
2. "Long Time Missing"
3. "No One in this City"
4. "Listen to Me"
5. "When Our Vows Break"
6. "Einstein's Day"
7. "Highwire Days"
8. "Big Blue Sky"
9. "Back to Zero Now"
10. "Places That Are Gone"

September 10, Theater of the Living Arts, Philadelphia, PA
Opening for Guided by Voices.

September 11, The 9:30 Club, Washington, DC
Opening for Guided by Voices.
Set List:
1. "Call on Me"
2. "Long Time Missing"
3. "No One in this City"
4. "Compromise"
5. "When Our Vows Break"
6. "Big Blue Sky"
7. "Einstein's Day"
8. "Highwire Days"
9. "Turning on Blue"
10. "Back to Zero Now"
11. "Places That Are Gone"
12. "Kill Your Sons"

November 11, Canes, San Diego, CA
Opening for Guided by Voices.

November 12, Spaceland, Los Angeles, CA

November 13, The Fillmore, San Francisco, CA
Opening for Guided by Voices.
Set List:

1. "Call on Me"
2. "Turning on Blue"
3. "No One in this City"
4. "Listen to Me"
5. "Good Thing Going"
6. "Einstein's Day"
7. "Big Blue Sky"
8. "Long Time Missing"
9. "Places That Are Gone"

2005

No known gigs.

2006

June 9, Spaceland, Los Angeles, CA
With John Richardson on drums, Paul Chastain (of Velvet Crush) on bass, and Dave Phillips (of the Robert Pollard band) on guitar.
Set List:
1. "Black and White New York"
2. "Turning on Blue"
3. "Warren in the '60s"
4. "Silent Town"
5. "Highwire Days"
6. "Lives Become Lies"
7. "Quit That Scene"
8. "My Mother Looked Like Marilyn Monroe"
9. "Driving Down the Road in My Mind"
10. "Compromise"
11. "Long Time Missing"
12. "Places That Are Gone"
Encore:
13. "Back to Zero Now"
14. "Kill Your Sons"

June 14, TT the Bears, Boston, MA

June 15, The M Room, Philadelphia, PA

June 16, Maxwell's, Hoboken, NJ

June 17, The Iota, Arlington, VA
Set List:
1. "Black and White New York"
2. "Turning on Blue"
3. "Warren in the '60s"
4. "Silent Town"
5. "Highwire Days"
6. "Lives Become Lies"
7. "Quit That Scene"
8. "My Mother Looked Like Marilyn Monroe"
9. "Einstein's Day"
10. "Driving Down the Road in My Mind"
11. "When Our Vows Break"
12. "Compromise"
13. "Long Time Missing"
14. "Places That Are Gone"
Encore:
15. "Back to Zero Now"
16. "Kill Your Sons"

June 20, Club Cafe, Pittsburgh, PA

June 21, Lager House, Detroit, MI

June 22, Schuba's, Chicago, IL
Opening for "Townshend Research," a pseudonym for the Robert Pollard band.
Set List:
1. "Black and White New York"
2. "Turning on Blue"
3. "Warren in the '60s"
4. "Silent Town"
5. "Highwire Days"
6. "Lives Become Lies"

7. "My Mother Looked Like Marilyn Monroe"
8. "Driving Down the Road in My Mind"
9. "Compromise"
10. "Long Time Missing"
11. "Places That Are Gone"
Encore:
12. "Kill Your Sons"

September 28, 400 Bar, Minneapolis, MN
Brad Quinn returns on bass.

September 29, The Beat Kitchen, Chicago, IL

September 30, Mad Planet, Milwaukee, WI

978-0-595-44770-1
0-595-44770-8

Lightning Source UK Ltd.
Milton Keynes UK
07 December 2009

147202UK00002B/128/A

Lightning Source UK Ltd.
Milton Keynes UK
07 December 2009

147202UK00002B/128/A